Y0-ARF-634

WALKS ON WESTON CONSERVATION LAND

A GUIDE

ELMER E. JONES

ILLUSTRATOR
CAROL GOVAN

WESTON, MASSACHUSETTS
1999

Publisher
Weston Forest and Trail Press
266 Glen Road, Weston, MA 02493
URL: http://www.weston-forest-trail.org

Layout/Cover/Production Editor:
Foley Engineering
Photography Tom Selldorff (front cover)
Photography Tom Seldorff (back cover)
Photography T. Seldorff and E. Jones (general)
Pen and ink illustrations: Carol Govan

Copyright © 1999 by Elmer E. Jones

All rights reserved.
No part of this publication may be reproduced
except for brief passages for review, without
written permission from the publisher.

First edition.
Printed in U.S.A.

ISBN 0-9672295-0-2

Library of Congress Catalog Card Number:
99-63997

As with any physical activity, good health
and or a doctors approval is assumed. The
author suggests beginning with the least
demanding walks.

ACKNOWLEDGMENTS

George Bates and Susan Dumaine critically read the manuscript for general interest and accuracy of trail description. Susan checked my botany. Francis Brooks, Leon Cohen, Lee Fernandez, Anna Melone Pollock and others read one or more chapters and made recommendations and supplied additional data. I owe a great deal to them for their input. I also owe a great debt to those who have asked questions when walking with me. I answered those questions to the best of my knowledge or sought an answer from the literature, friends or colleagues. Some of what I have learned appears with the trail descriptions in this book.

TABLE OF CONTENTS

GENESIS OF THIS GUIDE

In 1953, I went to Weston for the first time to visit my sister who was living on Hilltop Road. As it was our custom to talk and to walk together, we set out along the Massachusetts Central Branch of the Boston and Maine Railroad to find something new. In 1963, my wife, Alice, and I moved to Weston. We learned of many special places in Weston from our neighbors, especially Lee and Betty Rafuse and Charlotte Smith. When Charlotte felt that she could no longer lead the Spring Massachusetts Audubon Walk in Weston, she asked me to continue them which I did until about 1990. My wife served as a Conservation Commissioner from 1970 to 1995 and I serve as a Trustee of the Weston Forest and Trail Association. Both my wife and I taught science about forty years. In our spare time, we walked Weston looking for new discoveries

Over the years, friends suggested that I should write some of my informal talks down. Several starts were made before I retired from Northeastern University, but a busy schedule of lectures, talks, and walks made progress slow. My brother and one sister developed cancer that added to my duties. After the Faculty Laboratory and Office Building (FL0B) at the University of North Carolina Medical School at Chapel Hill was dedicated to the memory of my sister, Mary Ellen Jones, during the Spring of 1997, I concentrated on this book until it was complete. Thus, this book is dedicated to my sister who first introduced me to walking in Massachusetts and in Weston.

This book will be a success if it encourages you to use your senses to experience this world during your walks. My family, friends and teachers showed me that it is very easy to see a new phenomenon whenever you go forth on a little walk if you take along an active curiosity.

                              Elmer E. Jones

USING THIS GUIDE

This guide is to serve as an introduction to the conservation lands of Weston, Massachusetts. Each walk description begins with a section giving GENERAL INFORMATION about the locality. Next, a section suggests PARKING. The section RECOMMENDED WALK describes a walk as if you were accompanying the author as he points out interesting features and history of the locality. The guide is not exhaustive but is to serve only as an introduction to your further exploration.

The Weston Forest and Trail Association has published this guide and also a trail map of Conservation, Municipal, and Park Lands in the Town of Weston. The map may be purchased at the Conservation Commission office.

To facilitate orientation in the woods, several intersections have been marked with letters or numbers which are shown on the maps. Some house numbers are also shown to help in locating points of entry into the Conservation Lands.

Most of the trails described in this guide are on Town or other conservation land. Whenever a trail passes over private property, this will be noted in the description.

Trails are marked with aluminum markers that are painted white with a green pine tree surmounting a green W. These markers were donated to the Weston Forest and Trail Association by the Continental Can Company. The direction in which the tree symbol on the trail marker points has the following meaning:

Trail continues straight ahead

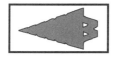

Trail turns to the left

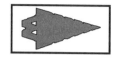

Trail turns to the lright

Trail ends or trail enters private property

Labled junction

In this Guide, these markers are referred to as F&T signs.

Let's begin

CAT ROCK
and
80 ACRES

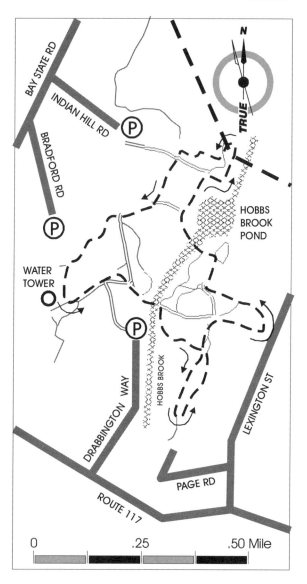

MAP 1

GENERAL INFORMATION:

Cat Rock and the adjacent 80 Acres Conservation Land have a total area of about 130 acres.

Cat Rock consists of 64.4 acres. The summit of Cat Rock is 334 feet above sea level and is lower than several other sites to the south. Doublet Hill's west summit is slightly higher than 360 feet and the marker on the east summit reads 356 feet. The site of the Revolutionary War Beacon on Sanderson Hill along Highland Street lies about 350 feet, and the Mt. Lemuel in the Pine Street Town Forest has a marker reading 356 feet. The ridge of Cat Rock runs roughly in the direction of flow of the glacier during the last glaciation which ended about ten thousand years ago. The glacial striations indicate that the glacier flowed southeast over our area.

The Cat Rock Area was purchased in 1957 by the Town of Weston from the Trustees of the Cat-Rock Trust. The Recreation Commission maintains the baseball field at the end of Drabbington Way. From 1957 through 1978, the Recreation Commission maintained a rope ski tow on Cat Rock. Lack of reliable snow during the winter and the cost of converting the crude rope tow to a system meeting present safety standards were among the reasons for closing the ski slope. William Martin Jr. wrote an article "Skiing at Cat Rock: Yesterday and Today", *The Weston Historical Society Bulletin*, XXVIII, 14,

Spring 1997 which describes some recent activity at Cat Rock.

80 Acres was the name given to the area north of Cat Rock by Frederic C. Dumaine, Jr. and Albert B. Hunt when they purchased this land. The first farmer was Abraham Sanderson who built the house at 178 Lexington Street in 1761. About 1830, the farm and homestead became the property of John Warren Cutting. Sometime after Mr. Cutting's death, the estate was sold to Sidney E. Tyler. In the late 1800's, the Tyler farm was noted for sweet corn that was exported to the Boston market. Herbert E. Tyler, Sidney's son, continued the farm and served Weston as a Selectman for 36 years from 1912 to 1948. His portrait was displayed on your left as you entered the Town Hall. In 1953, the farm was sold to Frederic C. Dumaine, Jr. and Albert B. Hunt. The two hundred year old farm house was rebuilt, a wet meadow was dammed to form Hobbs Pond, and the area was used as a wildlife sanctuary. During the mid-1970's, they deeded much of the land to the Town.

Hobbs Brook runs through these areas dropping from 135 feet at the Waltham/Weston border to 95 feet at North Avenue. It connects the Cambridge Reservoir with the Stony Brook Reservoir. The Cambridge Water Department controls the flow of Hobbs Brook between these reservoirs. These reservoirs supply water to Cambridge and were made by excavating and damming portions of the Hobbs and Stony

Brook drainages during the 1890's. Hobbs Brook takes its present name from Ebenzer Hobbs. In 1750, he built a tannery at the corner of North Avenue and Church Street. Thus, this road junction was known as Hobbs Corner. From about 1750 through 1860, the Hobbs family ran a tannery using Hobbs Brook as its water supply. During the winter months, many of local farmers made shoes from the tannery leather.

PARKING:
There are three convenient parking spots.

1) At the end of Drabbington Way, there is the parking lot for the Cat Rock Ball Field.

2) The circle at the end of Bradford Road provides a close approach to the summit of Cat Rock.

3) Indian Hill Road ends at a path leading to Hobbs Pond at 80 Acres.

RECOMMENDED WALK:
Starting from the Cat Rock Ball Field Parking Lot, follow the path to the right of the ball field fence to the fire road. Turn right on this road and cross the bridge over Hobbs Brook. During May, one should scan the trees along the brook for migrating warblers. Along the brook in May, one may find flowers belonging to the lily family - bellwort (*Uvularia perfoliata*) (Figure 1), Solomon's seal (*Polygonatum* sp.) (Figure 2), and wild spikenard or false Solomon's seal (*Smilacina*

racemosa) (Figure 3). During spring and summer, cinnamon fern (*Osumunda cinnamonea*) (Figure 4), interrupted fern (*Osumunda claytoniana*) (Figure 5), royal fern (*Osmunda regalis*)(Figure 6), and other ferns may be found along the brook. Just beyond the bridge, turn to your right leaving the fire road to follow a path through moist woodland to the edge of an overgrown dry meadow. You may either turn to your right making a loop along a path that returns to this spot or turn to the left following an old farm road. During May, this is a good birding area. Many warblers may be present including the blue-winged warbler.

Leaving the overgrown dry meadow along the old farm road, one soon encounters the fire road again. To your right, there is an old swimming pool built by the White family. Their estate occupied the land now belonging to the Cambridge School.

Turn right on the fire road and continue east toward Lexington Street. About 50 feet before the gate on Lexington Street, there is a path leaving the fire road on the left just before a large red oak. Follow this path across an overgrown meadow and pass through a stone wall. This path ends at a large glacial erractic where it meets an east-west path. A glacial erractic is a boulder transported by a glacier and then dropped when the glacier melted. There are several smaller erractics here. The path

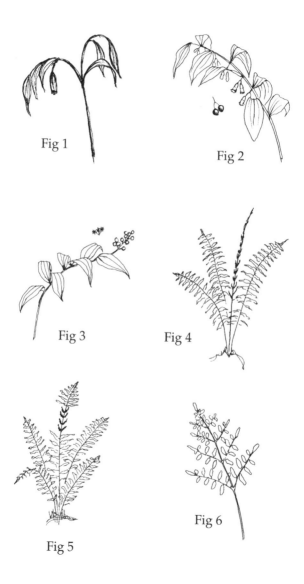

Fig 1

Fig 2

Fig 3

Fig 4

Fig 5

Fig 6

leading to your right goes over a bed rock outcrop before reaching Lexington Street and Georgian Road. To our north, there is a swamp that is a good place to look for ducks and marsh birds. During the summer, a green-backed heron may often be found.

Bear left from the glacial erractic. The path soon turns to the left and passes through a stone wall. Immediately turn right and follow along a stone wall to a wall corner where the path passes through the wall. The path bears right for about 20 feet and then turns to the left (west). In about 50 feet, the path ends on a fire road. The fire road ends at a dam. This dam was built in 1957 and rebuilt in 1994. During the spring, Canada geese and ducks may nest on the small islands in this pond. Often goslings and ducklings can be observed either on the pond or on the adjacent meadow during late May or early June.

Cross Hobbs Brook on the bridge just below the dam. The path returns you to the top of the dam where it becomes a road. Follow the road keeping close to the south edge and then the west edge of the pond. Soon, the road ends on a second road coming from the end of Indian Hill Road. Turn right and follow the road to the edge of the meadow. If you go straight ahead along the pond, the road enters onto private land by a bridge and one should respect the rights of the owners. At the meadow edge, you should pause to look over the pond. At the end of May, Baltimore orioles can be seen building their nests in the trees. Young goslings can be present either on the island, the pond, or along the meadow. Shorebirds may often be seen along the edge of the pond. Eastern painted turtles can be seen in late spring on warm and sunny days. Occasionally, one may see a snapping turtle.

At the edge of the meadow, turn left and head north on a path which leads to a stone wall. Upon reaching the stone wall, avoid the path going straight ahead, it goes to a site where GTE maintained a radar dish for many years. Take the path going to the left along the edge of the meadow. It soon passes through the wall to the right. The path passes along the base of a large bedrock outcrop. Avoid the path to your left that goes to the top of the outcrop and continue straight ahead to another stone wall that marks the Waltham/Weston border. Avoid the path to the right that goes to the former GTE radar site. Go to your left along the top of the outcrop, then the path drops down to your right passing through a wooded area before reaching an open meadow. Passing through this wooded area one may see great horned owls and deer in the early morning or at dusk.

Upon reaching the open meadow, turn to your left. If you turn to the right, the path soon reaches Waltham and eventually reaches the end of Kings Grant Road in Weston.

The path soon crosses the road from the end of Indian Hill Road. Continue straight south along the path that follows the meadow edge. Northern mockingbirds, brown thrashers, gray catbirds, and other open field species can be found here during the late spring and summer. At the end of the field, a path comes from your left from the dam and enters the woods. Go right on this path into the woods. It may be quite wet where this path passes through the stone wall. The intermittent stream just beyond the stone wall is usually dry in late summer and fall. This stream comes from a vernal pond to your right and flows to Hobbs Brook. Continue along the fire road that bears left and continues to the Cat Rock Ball Field. A stroll along this road and the paralleling path between late April and early June will usually reward you with displays of many of our common woodland flowers.

Where the fire road turns back to our starting point, on the right there is a scenic path to the summit of Cat Rock. Woodland flowers also are found along this path. The path brings you near the end of Bradford Road. From here, one can go to the water tower just below the summit of Cat Rock. The view to the north is commercial. Early in the 1960's, this northerly view overlooked mainly woodlands. The view point south of the water tank looks towards Regis College and Wellesley. You may notice the crescent of hills which lie in the south and western parts of Town and which are higher than Cat Rock.

Walking down the open ski slope returns you to the ball field and the parking lot.

NATURAL HISTORY NOTE: This area has been used by the Massachusetts Audubon Society for birding classes as the area presents a variety of habitats — hardwood areas, evergreen areas, open field and meadow, brushy borders, overgrown field, fresh-water marsh, stream sides, and an open pond. In March and April, woodcock courting flights may be observed near sunset. During the height of migration, it is easy to list more than 50 species here in a few hours. Often, great horned owl chicks can be observed in the tall pines during the spring. With luck, a parent owl may look you over as you stand watching its child. Mammals are more elusive. Rabbits are common; raccoons and possums are also present but harder to observe. Mice and voles are abundant during most years as can be judged from the constant presence of raptors. In some years, active fox dens can be found. In the late evening, deer can be found feeding on the open meadows.

NEARBY FEATURE OF INTEREST: About 25 feet east of the mailbox for 9 Legion Road, there is a large bedrock outcrop along the road. If you examine the surface of this outcrop, you can clearly see glacial polish and striae. Glacial polish is a satin-smooth finish produced by the scouring action of the overriding ice on the rock. Glacial striae are large scratches and grooves produced by the rocks frozen beneath the ice as they grind over the surface of the bedrock under the weight of the overlying ice. The round holes in the rock are drill holes. Apparently, the rock was to be blasted but for some reason has been spared.

Between twenty to ten thousand years ago, our area lay under about a mile of glacial ice. This ice sheet determined much of the gross topography of our landscape.

COBURN MEADOW

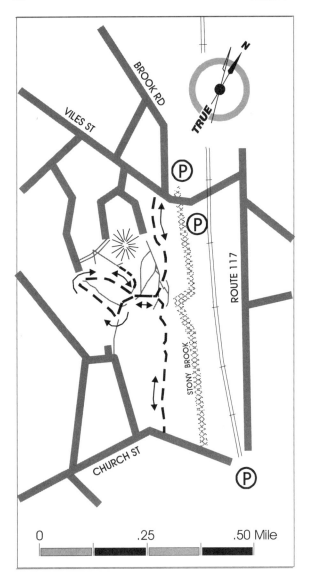

MAP 2

GENERAL INFORMATION:

The Coburn Meadow consists of 46 acres of town land plus 10 acres of Forest and Trail Association land. It lies in the Stony Brook drainage. This area was once a source of water for Weston and remains so for the City of Cambridge. The drainage extends from Beaver Pond, Flint's (Sandy) Pond, and Todd Pond in Lincoln to the Charles River. Cherry Brook that begins in the Jericho Town Forest runs north joining Stony Brook just west of Viles Street. The meadow that lies between Route 117 and the Fitchburg Division of the MBTA Commuter Rail Line was formerly known as Long Meadow; and, roughly from 1640 to 1950, was used for grazing and haying by local farmers.

The Coburn Meadow is bound on the southeast by Church Street and on the northeast by the Fitchburg Division of the MBTA Commuter Line. This railroad, situated on a level river terrace deposit, was built as the Fitchburg Railroad during the 1840's. Service from Kendal Green to Boston began in 1844. The railroad became a part of the Boston and Maine Railroad system about 1900. The commuter railroads in the Greater Boston Area came into the MBTA system during the late 1960's and the early 1970's.

South of the railroad lies a wet meadow which acts as a sink for flood waters of the Stony Brook Drainage. It is possible to canoe Stony Brook from Viles Street almost to the Kendal Green

Station during the warmer months of the year. Stony Brook is stocked with trout by the Commonwealth. Stocking attracts many sports fishermen and the occasional otter. During snowy winters when Stony Brook is mostly frozen over, the Hastings commuters on train 408 or 412 can be treated to the sight of an otter running along the frozen Stony Brook looking for an ice-free access to the brook and a meal.

The river terrace deposits are also found on the southwest edge of the Stony Brook valley. The row of six houses from 75 to 87 Brook Road were built for employees of the former Hastings and Hook Organ Company and are situated on this river terrace. In the area of Brook Road and Viles Street, these terraces are about 0.2 mile wide. Behind these houses, the land rises sharply to a further terrace on which Old Coach Road lies.

The Weston Golf Club was located in this area after it was first organized in 1894. The course had 9 holes. Holes 1,2,3,8, and 9 were located on the present conservation land. The other holes were located further to the west along Brook Road, Valley View Road, and Old Coach Road. To avoid competition with cows grazing on the first and third fairway, two of the greens were surrounded with iron pipe fences, which can still be observed along the trails. In 1917, the Weston Golf Club moved to its present location on Meadowbrook Road.

The land rises toward a bedrock exposure beyond Lantern Lane. To the southeast of this summit, there is a stream valley. This stream runs from the end of Fairview Road toward the wet Coburn meadow through a stand of very large hemlocks. At the end of the hemlock grove, the stream sinks into the ground at a marshy spot and emerges along the base of the embankment next to the wet meadow as a series of springs.

At the intersection of Viles Street and the MBTA Commuter Rail Line, was the site of Hastings Station. The present parking lot is located on the site of the station that burned about 1960. East of this intersection, behind a row of large maples (four remained in 1999) stood the Hastings and Hook Organ Factory. It was torn down in 1936 after radio and sound motion pictures had reduced the demand for do-it-yourself musical instruments. The organ of the First Parish Church in Weston is a Hastings and Hook organ. Also, at this site was the social center for employees, a railroad siding, and material storage areas. The two remaining duplex houses on the west side of Viles Street were organ factory housing. The garages on the east side of Viles Street provided storage for metals used in making the organs.

PARKING:
This area may be entered from many of the abutting streets. Convenient parking is found:

1) On Brook Road beside the Edward J. Czarnowski Ball Field.

2) At Kendal Green along the road to the Weston Recycling Area.

RECOMMENDED WALK:

Start from the Edward J. Czarnowski Ball Field at the junction of Brook Road and Viles Street, cross Viles, and pass through the stone gateway leading toward 77 Viles Street. Along the right hand side of the drive is a path marked with a F & T sign. Follow this path along the base of the slope keeping a house to your left. Next, you pass a marshy area to your right. The trail rises and passes a path going to your right. Continue straight passing through a stone wall and descend slightly until the path splits. Take the left hand path into a small overgrown meadow rather than the path going up the slope. During the 1960's, the neighborhood children referred to this meadow as "rabbit island". If you sit quietly here, you may see rabbits on the meadow and ducks, muskrats, and otters in the brook. Occasionally, grouse roost in the cedars in this area. Continue in the same direction along the path. You will pass through a gateway in a stone wall and then into an open meadow. From here, you can see the "Coburn Barn" on Church Street. You may walk to Church Street and parking spot 2 from here. The "Coburn Barn" is on private property that should be respected.

Returning to the meadow corner, retrace your steps back to "rabbit island" and pass through the stone wall. Turn right and walk along parallel to the wet meadow. Why are all those pipes along the path? Actually, there are two sets of pipes. The older set of one inch pipes are a fence erected by the original Weston Golf Club to keep the cows from trespassing on the greens of hole 1 and 3. The short, wide, and capped pipes are test wells drilled by the Weston Water Department in a search for water. The salting of the Massachusetts Turnpike Authority's toll plaza resulted in Weston's wells being saltier than the Dead Sea. The MWRA required the Town to search for a new water source within the town as a pre-condition of supplying MWRA water to the Town.

As we leave the area of pipes and just before passing through a stone wall, you will note an old cow path to your left which climbs the slope on a diagonal. Follow this cow path until you reach a wide trail. Turn left on this trail. Upon reaching a terrace, continue straight ignoring the crossing path. The crossing path goes, on the left, into private land; and, on the right, to the end of Old Coach Road.

The trail skirts a hole to your left and soon reaches a junction where a path climbs a hill. Bypass the uphill path keeping to your left and cross an intermittent stream. This stream soaks into the soil at a marshy spot to your left. The water later emerges at the foot of the terrace as a series of springs.

After crossing the stream, turn to your right and follow the path that parallels the stream. A grove of large hemlock trees grows in this protected, wet, and cool valley. When you are in sight of the house which blocks this valley, turn to your right when the path no longer seems to continue and recross the stream. (At times, there may be a bridge here.) Ignore the path heading to the right along the opposite side of the stream and take a path that climbs up the slope to the end of Pinecroft Road. Just before reaching Pinecroft Road, turn to your right and follow a path leading along the hillside. You may notice on the dry hillside that oaks and white pines predominate. Continue along the path which tends downhill until you reach a large glacial boulder on your left. The boulder is a glacial erratic; that is, a large boulder plucked by a glacier, transported along with the flowing ice, and dropped some distance from its origin as the glacier melted.

At the erratic, turn left onto a path that passes the erratic and a bedrock outcrop. Continue to the top of the hill which is a bedrock outcrop situated about 210 feet above sea level. In the winter, one can see across the valley to the Cat Rock water tank and to Hobbs Corner. Although the path continues west to the end of Lantern Lane, you should retrace your steps to the boulder and then turn left following the path down a slightly steep hillside. Upon reaching the terrace, continue straight ahead on the trail on which you came up the hill. Follow the trail back down to the river terrace and turn left to return to Viles Street.

HISTORICAL NOTES: Additional information on the Hastings and Hook Organ Factory may be found in the *The Weston Historical Society Bulletin* Vol. XVII, No. 1, pages 4 and 5 (1980); Vol. XVIII, No. 2, pages 6 and 7 (1982); Vol. XX, No. 1, pages 1 - 12 (1983); and Vol. XX, No. 2, pages 1 -10 (1984). The original Weston Golf Club at Kendal Green (1894 - 1917) is described by Philip F. Coburn in *Growing Up in Weston* on pages 22 - 25 with a map of the course appearing as a frontispiece.

Day lily seed head
(*Hemerocallis 'Stella de Oro'*)

THE
SEARS LAND

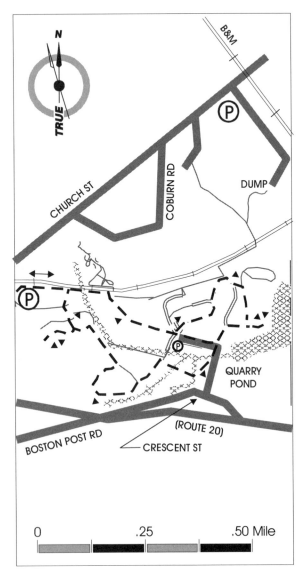

N

TRUE

B&M

P

CHURCH ST

COBURN RD

DUMP

P

P

QUARRY
POND

BOSTON POST RD

(ROUTE 20)

CRESCENT ST

| 0 | | .25 | | .50 Mile |

MAP 3

GENERAL INFORMATION:

In 1975, the "Sears" Conservation land was given to the Town by Edwin and Rosamond Sears. The gift of 61 acres plus two adjoining parcels of Town Land with an area of 21 acres form a total area of 82 acres of Conservation Land between the abandoned Massachusetts Central Railroad and Crescent Street.

The northerly boundary of the property is the abandoned railroad. The Wayland & Sudbury Railroad Company was chartered in 1868 to construct a seven mile line from the Fitchburg Railroad in Weston to South Sudbury. Before the ink was dry on the charter, the Massachusetts Central Railroad was chartered in 1869 to build a longer railroad from Weston to Northhampton along the route of the Wayland & Sudbury. Actual construction began from Weston in 1871. The contractor failed during the Panic of 1873; and construction was not resumed until 1878. By October 1881, one could travel 28 miles from Boston to Hudson; and by 1882, it was possible to travel to Jefferson, 46 miles from Boston. The railroad failed again in May 1883. In 1885, the railroad was reorganized as the Central Massachusetts Railroad and operation was taken over by the Boston and Lowell Railroad. In 1887, these railroads were absorbed by the Boston & Maine Railroad that completed the line to Northampton. From 1887 to 1893, the Boston & Maine Railroad used this route as its outlet to the west. Long distance service over this route ended in November 1893 and commuter service ended on November 26, 1971. This railroad gradually shrank from Northampton to Clinton (1932), to Berlin (1958), and finally to South Sudbury (1965). The last steam passenger trains in regular service in Massachusetts ran over these tracks being replaced in 1956 by rail diesel cars (RDCs). The RDCs were used until the end-of-service. Freight service continued until about 1980 on an as needed basis with speed restricted to 5 mph.

In *Random Recollections*, Brenton H. Dickson observes that looking at the Weston Station today and the unused track in front of it, one has little idea of the hustle and bustle that once characterized the place. He notes that, in 1916, when service reached its peak, twenty-three passenger trains stopped at the Weston Station every weekday as well as five scheduled freights. By 1955, when I commuted from Weston Station, there were only five passenger trains on weekdays and freight trains ran only as needed, usually once or twice a week.

The former quarry pits of the Massachusetts Broken Stone Company lie to the east of the Sears Land. Just to the west of the quarry, there was a wet meadow situated below the 100 foot contour. This meadow was flooded to form a shallow pond to supply process water for the quarry. Two brooks supply water to the pond. One of these brooks, Three Mile Brook, was an important source of water power for over two hundred years for mills once sited in this area.

A map showing the water shed of these brooks can be found in the Open Space & Recreation Planning Committee, *Open Space & Recreation Plan Resource Analysis for the Town of Weston, MA* (Revised Summer 1997), page 30.

From the 1920's until 1980, the land between Crescent Street and the abandoned railroad was farmed by the Melone family During these years, the Melone family occupied the house at 27 Crescent Street that is situated in a central location in this conservation area. North of this house lies a small hill with several bedrock outcrops. The oaks on this hill were damaged by the Gypsy Moth infestation of the late 1980's. These oaks were selectively cut for lumber and firewood by Land's Sake for the Conservation Commission. Sugar maples were left in the hope that these sugar maples will form a sugar bush away from the effect of road salt. The crest of this small hill lies at 190 feet. South of 27 Crescent Street lies a part of the wet meadow discussed in the last paragraph that lies above the 100 foot contour. Philip F. Coburn in *Growing Up in Weston* refers to this wet meadow as Blood's swamp. This name may have originated from the fact that, during the early 1900's, a Mr. Blood lived at 27 Crescent Street.

South of Blood's swamp, the land rises to 180 feet at the junction of the Boston Post Road and the Post Road By-pass. The original route of Three Mile Brook, now situated mostly under route 20, carried the brook into the pond just

north of the junction of the Boston Post Road
and the Post Road By-pass. In the half mile from
this pond to the pond behind Massachusetts
Broken Stone, Three Mile Brook drops 80 feet.
The energy available from this falling water
resulted in this area becoming the site of small
industries from 1745 until 1935.

A report of the Crescent Street Historic District
Committee relates the following:

Three Mile Brook, which runs just north of
Crescent Street and eventually joins Stony
Brook, provided the power for the mills which
contributed to the development of the homes
along this section of the Country Road.
(Author's note: Country Road was the original
route from Boston to Worcester and the west.
It was straightened in 1854 leaving Crescent
Street off the main route to the delight of the
Crescent Street residents. The road was
renamed Central Avenue and then; in 1927,
the Boston Post Road.) The importance of this
power source is evidenced in deed records,
which contain frequent references to the
transfer of water rights along the stream.

The first mill in the Crescent Street area was
initiated some time before 1743 when David
Sanderson purchased farmland and water
rights on the brook in this section. He
operated a grist mill until 1745 on the stream
and built a small lean-to there. In 1751, the
"privilege to turn water" was recorded in the

deed records, granting that right to Benjamin Peirce. Early writings indicate that the brook flowed rapidly at the point where it flowed under a bridge built on the later-closed road which had passed the first Peirce Tavern. (Author's note: This road which ran between 21 and 29 Crescent Street past 27 Crescent Street to Church Street was abandoned in the 1770's.)

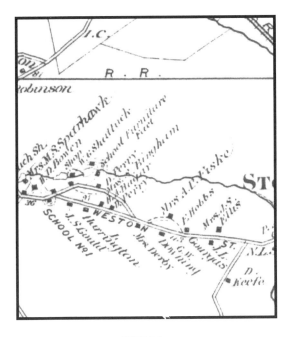

1874 Map
(Showing three factory sites)

The land behind the homes at 29, 39, and 49 Crescent Street provides a graphic example of the intricate waterways which were established to provide power for the early mills and factories. Still apparent are the remains of a dam, a millpond, and a canal for directing the water from Three Mile Brook. Large water wheels to power machinery were constructed here, and evidence of the supporting structure can still be seen.

In 1830, Samuel F. H. Bingham from Concord bought mill rights on Three Mile Brook and purchased land on what now is Crescent Street. In approximately 1838 - 1839, Bingham built the home at 39 Crescent Street. He also established a factory in the area behind this residence. Bingham made machinery for the manufacture of heavy woolen goods and invented the Bingham cheese and butter drill, a highly successful item which apparently was in great demand.

During this period, Samuel Shattuck used the quickly flowing stream water to provide power for a chair factory which he established at the point where Sanderson had initially built his mill. Shattuck's company prospered; upon his retirement in 1875, the firm was taken over by the Kenney Brothers and Wolkins, and later by Oliver M. Kenney alone, who specialized in school furniture, manufacturing both chairs and desks. The company was later acquired by George Perry, a member of a family which owned considerable land in the Crescent Street area. At the time of its operation, the factory, located downstream from Bingham's factory, used a water wheel 28 feet in diameter as a power source. Eventually needing greater waterpower, this successful operation moved to Baldwinville, Massachusetts in 1917. The wheel remained until approximately fifty years ago (Author's note: 1940's), providing an interesting landmark.

Records show that Bingham sold his "mill piece" in 1869 to an individual who sold the same piece to three businessmen Parker, Freeman, and Ross, in 1895. A year later, Charles Freeman bought out his partners, and subsequently operated the company as a screen factory. He produced window screens and door screens as well as weather stripping until 1933.

The factory was torn down about 1940.

The present Boston Post Road By-pass was built through Peat Meadow during the 1930's. Town records indicate that the manufacturer, Freeman, sued the selectmen for damages due to the impairment of his water rights because the By-pass acted as a series of dams across the brook and because the filling for the By-pass greatly reduced the water storage area of Peat Meadow. He was unsuccessful in his attempt to obtain compensation. Thus, it is difficult to see today that the present slow moving stream once had the capacity to drive factory wheels.

Besides the Hastings and Hook Organ Factory, the Hobbs Brook Tannery, and the factories of Three Mile Brook, there were also factories located in what is now the Stony Brook Reservoir and the Hews Pottery once located near Highland Street and the Boston Post Road. Industrial Weston died between 1890 and the 1930's except for Massachusetts Broken Stone. If you desire more information, I suggest consulting Col. Lamson's *History of Weston*.

PARKING:
There are three convenient parking spots.

1) At the Church Street Bridge, there is a parking lot in front of the former Weston Railroad Station.

2) One may drive up the old road between 21 and 29 Crescent Street and park just beyond 27 Crescent Street. Please respect the property at 27 Crescent Street.

3) From the parking lot at Kendal Green, one may take either of two routes.

   a) Follow the road into the Transfer Station Area keeping to the right. Walk up the ramp to the right of the truck scale and follow a trail over the top of the former landfill. After crossing a stone-lined drainage ditch on a bridge, the trail that is described below comes in from your right. Continue onto the former railroad bed. Turn to your right and walk along the railroad bed. The land to your left is the Sears Conservation Land and entrance trails are on your left. One trail leaves midway between the first and second high tension towers and a second leaves just beyond the second high tension tower. There are other trails further to the west.

b) Follow the sidewalk west along Church Street toward the Town Center. Just beyond the house at 171 Church Street, one reaches Hitching Post Lane. Turn left onto Hitching Post Lane; keep to the right side and enter Lower Field Road. The small ponds in this area have a nice display of water lilies during mid-summer. On your left, just before a sharp turn in Lower Field Road, there is a trail that follows the top of an esker. Take this trail. When you reach an old farm road that cuts into the esker near its end, turn left onto the old road which descends passing between two ponds. The trail rises and then descends into the area of the former landfill.

Descend and cross a stone-lined drainage ditch and walk up the slope of the former landfill. Head toward a high tension tower beside the former railroad bed. Just before you reach the railroad bed, a trail comes in from the left. Continue onto the former railroad bed. Turn to your right and walk along the railroad bed. The land to your left is the Sears Conservation Land and entrance trails are on your left. One trail leaves midway between the first and second high tension tower and a second leaves just beyond the second high tension tower. There are other trails further to the west.

RECOMMENDED WALK:

Start from the Weston Station by the Church Street Bridge and proceed east down the railway bed. Just after the second high tension tower (tower # 164), turn to your right and follow a well used path into the woods. Soon, an old road enters on your right which starts just above the railroad station and passes over private land. Go straight ahead along this old road which crosses a bridge into a hemlock grove. The road makes an "S" curve as it climbs through the hemlocks. The principal ground cover is partridgeberry (*Mitchella repens*) which blooms in the first week of July. Each ovary supports two flowers. Thus, if you examine one of the red berries, you may note "two belly buttons" at the bottom of each fruit. With a great deal of luck, you may find a ruffed grouse feeding here. Upon reaching a level spot, there is an orange "NO TRESPASSING" sign that is our notice to retrace our steps down the hill.

After reaching the bottom of the hill but before crossing the bridge, there is a F & T arrow sign on a path which goes to your right. Enter this path which passes through an ash grove and a stone wall before ending on a path. Turn right on this path. You will soon reach a stone wall that ranges from 6 to 8 feet in width. This wide wall runs east about 250 feet from the wall corner to your right. Why would one build a wall like this one? Actually the builder built two parallel walls four feet apart. As the farmer worked his field, he would dig or plow up many stones which were piled in a convenient spot. When winter arrived, he would pile the stones into a stone boat, a type of sled, and slide them to the space between the walls for dumping. Oxen rather than horses were used for this heavy hauling. During the 1960's when I first visited this area, there were the remains of very old apple trees on the upper part of the slope. Anna Melone Pollock told me that her father used this field to graze horses during the late 1930's and into the 1950's. We guessed that the apple orchard may have been maintained by Mr. Blood as the house at 27 Crescent Street was filled with apples when her father first found it.

Cross over the wall and walk up the hill keeping to your right along the edge of the meadow.

Rather than following the path to your left across the meadow, keep to your right along a marked path into the brush. This path ends on a road behind the large house at the junction of the Boston Post Road and its By-pass. Note the structure at the end of the pond. It is the foundation of a former machine shop. Turn to your left and follow this road along Three Mile Brook for a few minutes. Just after passing the path that runs across the meadow to your left, you will note to your right a short path that leads to a bridge at the end of an old mill pond. This was the site of water powered mills from 1751 until 1933. The screen factory on this site was removed in about 1940. The view to the east from this bridge looks down a ravine that was one of the outlets from the glacial Lake Sudbury.

Return to the road and continue downhill to a wall corner near a wetland and a brook. Turn to your right along a path keeping the wetland to your left. Just after the path takes a "U" turn, you will be looking up the ravine that was viewed from the bridge. Cross the bridge here and continue up the slope where you find a small mill pond. This mill pond and the mill race which exits from the pond are on private property. Turn to your left just before reaching the mill pond and follow a path which leads through the wood. The path soon reaches the mill race where it parallels the road from Crescent Street to 27 Crescent Street. Follow the mill race to its end near a concrete distribution box that once supplied water to the mill.

Drop down the bank to the paved road. Note the mill foundations to your left as you follow the road north. There was a 28 foot undershot water wheel on the brook just north of this site that was removed in the 1940's. The stone foundation for this wheel can still be seen on the south side of the brook just west of where the brook passes under the paved road. There probably was a mill at this site from 1745 until at least 1917.

Follow the paved road turning left and continue
to where the road ends in front of a house
located roughly in the center of this
conservation land. This house is numbered as 27
Crescent Street and is of uncertain origin. Note
that there is no door facing the road, but there
are entrances on the east and west sides and on
the back. Thus, we may guess that the house
was built as a multifamily house. Edwin B.
Sears, whose family owned 21, 27 (this house),
and 29 Crescent Street, believed that the house
was built by Shattuck who owned the mill
referred to above.

The house is now referred to as the Melone
Homestead by the Conservation Commission.
Mr. Joseph Melone came to the United States in
1921. He lived in Waltham and worked in
Weston digging foundations for many homes
built in the early 1920's, building the present
Town Green, and eventually becoming a
landscape worker on the Sears estate. He found
this disused and uninhabitable building in the
woods. With the Sears blessing, he, his wife,
Maria Anna, and young sons, Vincent and
William, renovated the house to provide a
family home. From 1921 until 1979, Mr. Melone
farmed the surrounding land as a subsistence
farm for his family as well as supplying fresh
vegetables to the Sears family. In return, the
Sears family granted a life tenancy in the farm to
Joseph and Maria Anna Melone. To the west of
the house stood a large barn and several out
buildings that have been removed since 1980.

Maria Anna maintained a vegetable garden here until her death in 1989. The eight Melone children excelled in Weston schools.

Land's Sake maintains an office in the Melone Homestead. Adjacent is a greenhouse where plants are started for setting out on the Town Muncipal Purpose Lands.

Follow the road that is just north of the house over the hill to an open area. Along the way, there is a series of descriptive signs, placed by Land's Sake, explaining their role in maintaining Weston's Conservation Land for the Conservation Commission. The signs were placed here in 1991 when Land's Sake harvested oaks in this area.

Upon reaching an open area within sight of the abandoned railroad track, turn to your right along a fire road. Continue east through an opening in the trees, pass a meadow on your right, cross a former farm road, and head south on a path which runs along the top of a ridge which overlooks a pond. This pond was formed when Massachusetts Broken Stone dammed Three Mile Brook to obtain a supply of process water for their operations. The pond is quite shallow and supports a considerable wildlife population. It is worth a visit almost anytime of the year.

At the end of the ridge, turn to your left and descend to pond level to see what can be observed. When the pond is ice free, one usually can find several species of ducks feeding. Once, in mid-May, a group of Weston bird watchers was treated to a show by a pair of otters and their two pups. Return to the top of the ridge and continue along a path to a woods road. Go down hill to your left and through an iron gate. In late April, just to the left of this gate, one may find bloodroot (*Sanguinaria canadensis*) (Figure 7), in bloom.

Fig 7

After passing through the gate, turn to your right along the road from Crescent Street, pass the Melone Homestead at 27 Crescent Street, and walk through the parking lot toward the Land's Sake greenhouse. Keeping the green house to your left head toward a high tension tower along the abandoned railroad. Once you reach the railroad, turn to your left and return to the station where the walk began.

NATURAL HISTORY: This area presents a variety of habitats: hardwood areas, evergreen areas, open field and meadow, brushy borders, fresh water marsh, stream banks, and an open pond. During the height of spring migration, it is easy to list more than 50 species of birds in a few hours. Often, great horned owl chicks can be observed in the tall pines in the spring. Most of the summer, a red-tailed hawk may be found perched on the top of one of the high tension towers.

Mammals are more elusive. Rabbits are common. Mice and voles are abundant most years as can be judged from the constant presence of raptors.

WALK

4

FORBES
CONSERVATION
LAND

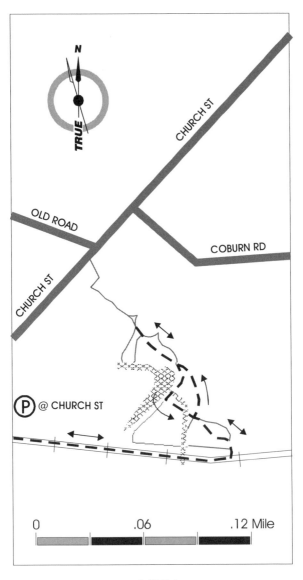

MAP 4

GENERAL INFORMATION:
In 1985, Celeste Forbes gave this parcel of land to the Town of Weston. Celeste Forbes, a founding member of the Weston Garden Club, inspired the club's 1992 renovation of the trails and rebuilding of the bridges on the property. The club also placed signs discussing the various habitat types, and labeled many of the plants that remain from Celeste and Mac Forbes' garden.

PARKING:
The most convenient parking place is at the former Weston Station at the Church Street bridge.

RECOMMENDED WALK:
Start from the Weston Station and go east along the former railroad. At the east end of the fill and about 75 feet before the third high tension tower east of the station, turn left and follow a path into the woods to a 5 foot long sign reading:

**FORBES CONSERVATION LAND
TOWN OF WESTON**

Follow the trail into the woods for roughly 30 feet, here there is a sign on a post which reads:

FORBES CONSERVATION LAND

In   1985,   Celeste   Forbes   gave   this conservation land to the town in order that "residents of Weston and their guests may view and enjoy the wildflowers and the wildlife present." Trails that Celeste and Mac Forbes laid out enable one to gain an intimate appreciation of the plants and animals that live in the mixture of upland woods and wet bottom land which is so common in our town.

Celeste Forbes, a founding member of the Weston Garden Club, inspired the club's 1992 renovation of the trails and bridges on the property.

The bridges were made by Land's Sake with wood grown and milled on the Sears land across the railroad tracks.

Go downhill keeping to your left and pass through a stone wall near a second sign at the edge between the dry upland and the wetland. This area may be very wet at times of high water. This second sign reads:

FORBES CONSERVATION LAND

The sloping area to the right of the path is on an upland woodland.

Topsoil on these slopes is dry, but rich in humus. Red oak and white pine are common, as are grey squirrel and chipmunk.

Further along the upland path (the path to your right), the large depression to the right is a "borrow pit." Soil was "borrowed" in

1871 to help make the Massachusetts Central Railroad.

The bottom land to the left is a vegetated wetland.

HOW IS A WETLAND IDENTIFIED?

Certain plants that are able to grow and reproduce in wet environments must be present. Vegetated wetlands are areas where more than half the plant cover ranges from species obligated to live in the water to those tolerant of soggy soil.

Some examples of wetland plants are: skunk cabbage, cinnamon fern, spicebush, red maple, and highbush blueberry.

WHY ARE WETLANDS VALUABLE?

Vegetated wetlands absorb and degrade many pollutants, recharge ground water essential for private and public water supplies, control flooding, and aid in reducing storm damage.

They are also essential for the survival of many types of plants and animal species.

And as you learn when standing here and observing with all your senses, the wetlands enrich the life of our own species as well.

As you face the sign, go to your left along the wetland and then slightly uphill. Within 30 feet you may find at the end of a stone wall a plant label reading:

Ironwood
Carpinus roliniana

Alternative names for this tree are American hornbeam, blue beech, musclewood, and water beech. The ironwood has a smooth grey bark with a sinewy appearance as if it had been doing muscle building exercises. There are many ironwoods in this area. The tree was prized by our forebears as its timber is exceptionally strong and was used for handles and levers. Two great naturalists living a century apart noted other applications: Pehr Kalm wrote that it was used for cart axles and as a premium grade fuel, and Thoreau observed that Indians made it into canoe paddles.

Another 30 feet and you will be overlooking the "borrow pit". Soil and gravel from the borrow pit were used by the railroad construction crews to fill the valley to the south. Note the width of the valley. It is an outlet from one of the glacial melt water lakes, Lake Sudbury. A second borrow pit is at the west end of the fill area. Such pits may be found all along the right of way of railroads wherever fill was required to establish the railroad grade.

The trail drops down to the wetlands and you will soon come to a junction. If you go straight ahead, the trail leads straight out to Church Street, along the way there is a side trail that leads down to the brook. If the black flies or mosquitoes will allow, you may wish to walk out almost to Church Street and then return to this point. Many of the plants are labelled in this area. In any case, you should turn and cross the bridge to a third sign that reads:

FORBES CONSERVATION LAND

TYPES OF WETLAND PRESENT:

SWAMP: A wetland dominated with trees and shrubs. Most of the wet portion of the Forbes Land is swampy. Water tolerant red maple with its red (female) or orange (male) flowers, red or green keys and brilliant fall foliage, early blooming spicebush with its fragrant bark and small yellow flowers, and the red-barked red osier dogwood thrive here.

MARSH: A wetland where herbaceous plants that thrive while standing in water predominate. Plants at the border of the pond form a mini-marsh.

POND: An open area of water such as that in front of you. During the spring and after storms, water fills the pond. Plants that need to have their roots in the water are found. Amphibians are common. Skunk cabbage hoods, and peepers announce the spring. Purple loosestrife blooms in the summer, while redwings call and tadpoles hurry to become frogs. In the late summer the pond surface dries, but the subsoil stays wet.

BROOK: The brook is a runoff from the Cherry Brook drainage system.

You may wish to walk to the end of the pond and return to this spot. Facing the sign, take the path behind you which goes through a part of the wetland and over a second bridge. In May, there are many interesting wildflowers to be seen along this path. After crossing the second bridge, go straight ahead to the top of the hill and return along the railway bed to the starting point.

WALK

5

CASE
MUNICIPAL PURPOSES
LAND

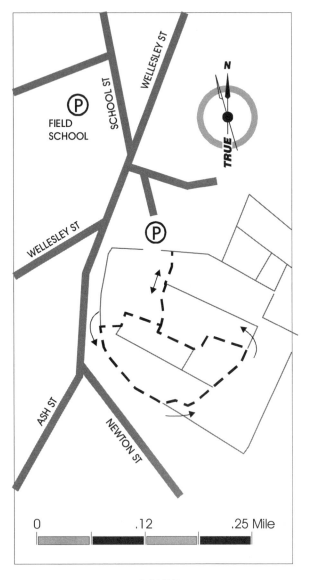

MAP 5

GENERAL INFORMATION:

The Case Municipal Purposes Land is owned by the Town of Weston, managed under the stewardship of the Weston Conservation Commission, and farmed by Land's Sake, a private non-profit organization. Its area is about 48 acres.

In 1909, Miss Marian Roby Case started Hillcrest Gardens on the fields now farmed by Land's Sake. Hillcrest Gardens was a practical school of agriculture and gardening open to boys of Weston and the surrounding towns. In 1911, Miss Case wrote "Hillcrest is an experimental farm where we wish to work up the scientific side of agriculture as well as to employ boys of the town through their long summer vacation." The boys worked in the fields here during the mornings; and, then in the afternoon, studied in classes held elsewhere on the Case Estate. The school operated from 1910 until 1943. In 1944, Miss Case willed all of her land to Arnold Arboretum. In 1986, the Town purchased this area from Harvard University as it had purchased other areas of the Case estate from Harvard for schools and the town pool during the late 1940's and in 1957.

Further information concerning the Case Family and Hillcrest Gardens (or Farm) may be found in *The Weston Historical Society Bulletin*, XVIII(4), May 1982 and *ibid.*, XIX(1), October 1982. A discussion of the Case Family and of the Weston part of the Arnold Arboretum is found in the interview with Dr. Donald Wyman among the oral histories kept at the reference desk of the Weston Public Library.

PARKING:
Use the parking lot at the junction of Newton and Wellesley Streets for the Land's Sake Garden.

RECOMMENDED WALK:
During this walk, we shall consider some plantings of the Arnold Arboretum, an interesting small marsh, and some geology. Many of the trees are experimental plantings of the Arnold Arboretum. These trees are mainly from the Orient and were planted in Weston to test their hardiness. Since Weston's winter temperature averages about ten degrees cooler than at the Arnold Arboretum in Jamaica Plain, any tree that could survive several Weston winters would thrive in Jamaica Plain.

From the parking lot, walk just past the farm stand and look towards Newton Street. You should notice several flat terraces one above the other.These flat terraces are former beaches of Lake Sudbury. Lake Sudbury was a glacial meltwater lake which formed as the glacier wasted away about ten thousand years ago. The Lake ran from what is now the Wayland border east to Green Lane. There are several spillways from this former lake which can be seen in this vicinity.   Head left to the large Norway maple behind the farm stand. A native of European forests, the Norway maple (*Acer platanoides*) closely resembles North America's sugar maple in leaf shape and habit. The easiest way to distinguish between the two species at a distance is to observe the bark. At maturity, the surface of a sugar maple's trunk is somewhat scaly, patchy, or peeling, and often displays a faint pink or orange tint. On the other hand, the surface of a Norway maple's trunk is more regularly furrowed vertically ridged bark. At closer range, there is a simple test. Remove a leaf from the sugar maple and it bleeds a clear sap; while a leaf removed from a Norway maple bleeds a milky sap. In this country, the Norway maple's role is chiefly as an attractive shade tree. However, Nina Danforth, who is a native Westonian, environmental educator, and a founding Trustee of Land's Sake, reports that the Norway maple is considered a pest in Massachusetts. She states that Norway maples spread rapidly to the edges of mowed areas killing out any native vegetation present. As the Norway maple has a dense shade, it prevents grass and other plants from growing. This maple does not turn brilliant colors in the fall as do our native maples. In Europe, its hard wood is used for furniture and the bark has been used for a reddish-brown dye.

Turn to your right and continue about 100 feet along a path parallel with the edge of a garden. On your right, there are six Korean mountain ashes *(Sorbus alnifolia)*. This tree flowers in May and develops showy pinkish red, orangish red,

or scarlet fruit in the fall. To your right about 25
feet further on, there is a pair of Japanese
pagoda or scholar trees (*Styphnolobrium
japonicum*, formerly *Sophora japonica*). These trees
are taller than the mountain ash and have
alternate compound leaves with 7 to 17 ovate
leaflets per stem. As its name suggests, the
pagoda tree is found around Buddhist temples.
Flowering during July through mid-August, it is
one of the last trees to flower in our area.

On your left between the pagoda trees is a
weeping willow (*Salix elegantissima*). There are
about 75 species of willow in North America
and they hybridize freely so it is difficult to be
sure which species or hybrid one is observing.

Passing between the pagoda trees keeping the
large spruce to your left, you come to three
golden larches (*Pseudolarix amabilis*). This tree, a
native of China where it grows at altitudes of
3000 to 4000 feet, was introduced into the United
States in 1854. Larches are members of the
conifer family that lose all their needles each fall
and remain bare throughout the winter. Most
pine trees develop new needles each year and
then shed their two year old needles in the fall
so that they are never bare. See how the needles
of the golden larch spread like fans from spur-
like branches and note that on the underside
you can see two grey bands of stomata, the tiny
pores that admit atmospheric gases into the leaf.
About mid-October, the light green leaves turn a
clear golden yellow. This fall color is brief but

wonderful. Dr. Donald Wyman noted that these trees are often as wide as they are tall.

As you near the stone wall along Newton Street, you can walk into the center of a group of six dawn redwoods (*Metasequoia glyptostroboides*). This tree, like the larches, drops its needles each fall and, like the gingko tree, can be considered a "living fossil". From about 90 to 15 million years ago, through the last of the Age of the Dinosaurs and well into the Age of the Mammals, this tree was one of the most prevalent conifers in the North Hemisphere. When the climate was less harsh, it even grew in the Arctic. About 15 million years ago, the cooling climate and a change in rainy seasons caused the dawn redwood's range to shrink tremendously, until it became restricted in modern times to one small area in eastern Szechwan and western Hupeh, China. The genus was first described by Miki in 1941 from a fossil discovered in Japan in Lower Pliocene strata. In the same year, a small population of this species was found living in a remote valley in central China. In 1947, Arnold Arboretum funded Chinese botanists who found metasequoia seeds and sent them to Boston in January 1948. These seeds were distributed to arboreta and botanical gardens throughout the world. Thus, this species has been reestablished throughout North America during the last 50 years. Its fall color may be described as pink, orange-brown, or red-brown. Its closest kin is the bald cypress with which it shares many traits. Both trees grow in a feathery-pyramidal habit, prefer wet soil, are somewhat salt tolerant, and lose their leaves in the fall.

A digression is required at this point. First graders know that the Mesozoic Era (245 to 65 million years ago) was the Age of Dinosaurs. During the first period of this Era, the Triassic, New England was snug in the heart of Pangaea, a supercontinent. At the onset of the second period, the Jurassic, a rift developed that became the present Atlantic Ocean. The dominate plants at this time were the gymnosperms which produce "naked" seeds which are not enclosed in a fruit. During the Mesozoic, four main types of gymnosperms were present: conifers (the cone bearing ancestors of modern pines, spruces, and redwoods); ginkophytes (one species survives as a "living fossil"); cycads (several species such as the sago palm still survive elsewhere in the world); and the extinct cycadeoids. Fossils of some of these plants, as well as dinosaur footprints, are preserved in the sedimentary rocks of the Connecticut River Valley in Massachusetts and Connecticut. In the final period of this Era, the Cretaceous, the first of modern flowering plants developed. Some flowering plants such as the grasses, which include our cereals, appeared during the Cenozoic Era (65 million years ago to the present). With this development, many of the browsing animals were replaced by grazers. Thus, this planet evolved into a suitable habitat for the development of mankind.

Continuing our digression, the gingko is not represented on this part of the Case Land.

However, a gingko or maidenhair tree (*Gingko biloba*) can be found across the street at the back of the island in the parking lot between Field School and the Library. It is one of the oldest of trees and has been growing on earth for 150 million years. Some paleobotanists believe that the gingko is the oldest genus of plant still living. Its leaves, which turn yellow in the fall, are unusual in that the veins start at the base of the leaf and then fan out in a series of dichotomous branches to the edge of the leaf (Figure 8). Remember the gingko is a gymnosperm and is more closely related to the pines than to the broad-leaved angiosperms. The angiosperms have a

Fig 8

Fig **9**

more hierarchical network of major and subsidiary veins that can be observed on any green shrub or tree leaf (See Figure 9: maple leaf) and compare with those of the gingko leaf.

The gingko is free of pests and diseases, but subject to air pollution. The tree is tolerant of poor soil as it forms a symbiotic relationship with actinomycetes, a bacterium that helps its roots to fix crucial nitrogen from nutrient-poor soil. Present research indicates that gingko may be medicinally useful as a treatment for asthma, toxic shock, memory problems, and blood problems. The gingko is dioecious, with separate female and male trees. It has a prolonged reproductive cycle as the five months between pollination and fertilization are followed by nine months of seed maturation. The seeds on the female tree resemble apricots (translation of the Chinese term gingko is silver apricot) but are not true fruits being simply seeds enclosed in a thin fleshy coat. When the seeds fall to the ground and begin to rot, they smell like rancid butter or very dirty athletic sox; thus, the male tree is preferred for ornamental plantings.

Leaving our digression to return to your walk, to the right of the dawn redwoods is a *Magnolia kobus* labelled "Wada's Memory". This magnolia was grown by C. S. Sargent of the Arnold Arboretum. It has six inch white flowers in late April. Flowering is followed by the emergence of bronze foliage that soon turns to dark green before turning rich yellow in the fall. There is unlabelled magnolia on the Wellesley Street side of the dawn redwoods that blooms in late April. The flowers have 15 white petals and are considered by some to be the most beautiful of the magnolias. This tree is probably a 'Merrill' magnolia that was raised from seed sown in 1939 at the Arnold Arboretum. This hybrid (*Magnolia x loebneri*) is the result of a cross between *M. korbu*s and *M stellata*.

About 75 feet beyond the magnolia, near the junction of Newton and Wellesley Streets, are a group of sourwoods (*Oxydendron arboretum*). Sourwood, a member of the heath family, is also called the sorrel tree or the lily-of-the-valley tree. It is a native of southeastern United States. Its flowers are white urn shaped, about a quarter of an inch long, and bloom in June to early July. In fall, its leaves turn yellow, red, and purple; often all colors appear on the same tree. Also, in this area, there is a collection of grafted cultivars of the Higan cherry (*Prunis subhirtella*) which bear flowers with a delicate lavender color in April.

Reverse direction and head back past the dawn redwoods and along the stone wall next to Newton Street, you will pass between two "Sunburst" honey locusts (*Gleditsia triacanthus* "Sunburst") and then to the right of three mountain ash (*Sorbus rosaceae*).

Just beyond the mountain ash lies a small wetland below a spring. The Case family had the water from this spring piped under Wellesley Street to their houses. For safety reasons, the well was filled in 1994. The delicate marsh fern (*Thelypteris palustris*) is found in this small marsh. Also, one may find grasses (the grass family has about 10,000 species worldwide), a rush (the rush family has about 400 species worldwide), and sedges (the sedge family has about 4000 species worldwide). The grass family (Gramineae) is recognized by certain characteristics: Grasses have narrow leaves with parallel veins and small inconspicuous flowers that are arranged in two rows. Grass stems are usually round and hollow except at the joints, easily visible bulges, where the leaves attach. Think of the 1960s' counterculture jargon, "grass means joint" and you will never forget how to recognize a grass. The long thin blades are those of soft rush (*Juncus effusus*). Rushes are recognized by the facts that the round leaves lack joints, the flowers are like tiny lilies with three petals and three sepals arranged in a circle, and the fruit is a small three-parted capsule that remains on the plant for most of the season. Rushes tend to grow in cool, wet areas such as this seep. Sedges, like rushes, tend to grow in cool, wet areas and their stems lack joints; however, the stems of a sedge are mainly solid and often triangular, "sedges have edges" and the flowers are arranged spirally on the stalk. I bet you can rapidly find several sedges in this small area and distinguish them from the many grasses.

Next, you will come to the curious "Temple's Upright" sugar maple (*Acer saccharum*

"Monumentale") with its very short branches. It often harbors several bird nests that can be seen in the fall after the leaves have dropped. Just to the right of this columnar sugar maple is an American sugar maple (*Acer saccharum*) with its spreading shape and orange bark.

To the left of the columnar sugar maple, there is a group of four Washington hawthorns (*Crataegus phaenopyrum*). These are broadly oval to rounded, dense, thorny trees. As the leaves unfold, they are reddish purple changing to dark green at maturity; fall color varies from orange to scarlet through purple. These trees flower in June. The fruit colors to a glossy red in the fall. The fruit persists all winter which makes it a nutritious food for birds.

About 50 feet ahead and to your right, there are four Carolina silverbells (*Halesia monticola*). This tree which is native to our southeast has a wonderful white, rarely pale pink or rose, bell-like flowers lasting about two weeks from late April into early May. The flowers emerge just before the leaves. In late summer, the fruit forms as a green ovoid four-winged drupe that eventually turns brown. The appearance of the fruit leads to this tree also being called the "Green Olive". Rhododendrons grow well under silverbells in our southern woods. The combination makes an outstanding spring display.

Looking down the slope, you will see a grove of nine Kurile Dahurian larches (*Larix gmelinii japonica*) with fine deciduous needles that turn golden in the fall before they drop.

You should now turn away from Newton Street and head for the spectacular European beeches that were planted by Mr. and Mrs. John Case in the 1870's. The first beech is a cut-leafed variety (*Fagus sylvatica laciniata*). Look at the leaves to see that 7 to 9 deep serrations on each side extend one-third of the distance from the edge to the midrib. Interestingly, the degree of serration varies on any one tree with the leaves at the top being more serrated than those at the bottom. One might guess that this pattern allows more light to reach the bottom leaves. Thus, the tree can capture more energy from the sun. Clones of the central tree arise from the roots to form a ring of smaller trees about the central trunk. When the central trunk dies, one of its clones will become predominate. Enter into the chamber about the main trunk and enjoy a wonderful green cathedral.

The second beech is a copper beech (*Fagus sylvatica purpurea*). The young leaves are a deep red-black and with time change to purple-green, and, in some cases, eventually turn green.

Leave the beeches and walk downhill between a blueberry patch at your left and a raspberry patch on your right and head straight along a farm road. To the left of the pine stand, there is a weeping Sargent's cherry (*Prunus sargentii*). Its leaves are tinged red as they emerge, become shiny dark green in summer, and range from yellow to bronze to red in the fall. From late April to early May, its flowers are single pink blossoms ranging up to one and a half inches across and they open before the leaves appear.

Continue along the road heading towards the magnificent, lone Scots pine (*Pinus sylvestris*). The needles occur in pairs and persist about three years. Note that the branches have a distinct orange-yellow bark.

Fig 10

Before passing the pine, turn left towards Newton Street and continue to the spreading silver linden (*Tilia tomentosa horizontalis*). This tree flowers in late June to early July. The yellowish-white flowers are very fragrant and are borne in 7 to 10 flowered pendulous, long cymes. A cyme (Figure 10) is a broad, loose and flat cluster of flowers. Some people are allergic to the fragrance or the pollen of the lindens.

Just beyond is a bigleaf linden (*Tilia platyphyllos compacta*) which flowers in early June. Its yellowish-white flowers are also very fragrant and are borne in 3-flowered, sometimes 6-flowered, pendant short cymes.

Return to the farm road and head back to the farm stand repassing many of the trees that we have admired. A bee keeper maintains his hives on this land and supplies Land's Sake with honey. Many of the flowering trees (cherries, crabapples, hawthorns, lindens, as well as others) supply the bees with a good supply of pollen and nectar.

WALK

6

DOUBLET HILL,
HEMLOCK POND AND
ELLISTON WOODS

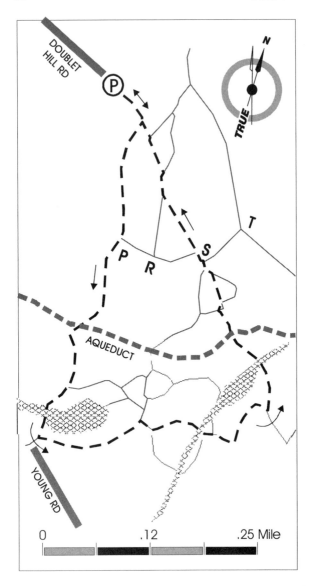

MAP 6

GENERAL INFORMATION:
The Doublet Hill conservation lands have an area of 35 acres and are separated from Elliston Woods and Hemlock Pond by the Weston Aqueduct. The Elliston Woods and Hemlock Pond have a total area of 25 acres.

Much of this area consists of bedrock outcrops with a veneer of glacial till. Glacial till is unsorted and unstratified stuff deposited directly from melting ice without resorting or reworking by streams. A bedrock exposure separates Hemlock Pond from the valley of Elliston Woods.

PARKING:
There is limited parking access to this area.

1) There is a cul-de-sac at the end of Doublet Hill Road. The walk described below begins at this cul-de-sac.

2) There is an access north of 44 Young Road.

RECOMMENDED WALK:
During this walk, we will look for changes that occur in the flora as we move down a hill from dry to wet habitats and then back up the hill.

From the cul-de-sac at the end of Doublet Hill Road, pass around the gate and go along a path. In about 200 feet you will come to a junction where several paths fan out. Take the path leading to your right. In this area the woods are largely a hickory/red oak forest. This type of forest is the common forest of the drier slopes of southern New England. The oldest trees are about 60 years old as much of the forest has grown up since the woods were uprooted in the 1938 hurricane and the farms were abandoned in the 1940's. At the height of land we pass between the two summits of Doublet Hill. The western summit lies on private property on your right, is just over 360 feet above sea level, and is the highest point in Weston. Later, we will return over the eastern summit which lies only a few feet lower.

As we start to descend, we reach an old road. To our left is a bedrock face that was cut by erosion. The path leaves the road, follows along this bedrock face, and rises as it leads south. Many of the low understory shrubs and trees growing along the path by this rock face are witch hazel,

Fig 11

winter-bloom, or snapping-alder (*Hamamelis virginiana*). The time to visit a witch hazel grove is in the fall about two weeks after the trees have shed their symmetrical, wavy edged leaves (Figure 11). The bare branches will be covered with spidery light-yellow blossoms that often last from mid-October into mid-December. If there is a freeze during this time, the petals roll up to avoid damage. The seeds require a year to mature so seed capsules are present along the branches at all times of the year. The capsules are about one-half inch long and contain one or two shiny black seeds that resemble a rice grain. As the capsules dry in the fall, they split open at the top projecting the seed with an audible pop. The seeds are dispersed at a distance from the parent plant. Authors differ on how far the seeds are dispersed with estimates ranging from five to forty feet. One result of this dispersion is that it is rare to find an isolated witch hazel. Its branches are used as "divining rods" by dowsers who search for minerals and water. The oil from the bark has long been recovered by steam distillation to be used as a cure for bodily ills.

Leaving the witch hazel grove, the path descends and passes through an area with many glacial erratics. A glacial erratic is a detached rock that has been borne from its point of origin by a moving glacier. Next, the path reaches junction **P** at the west terminus of a path that runs through the woods to the east. By this junction, there is an outcrop to your right. On the top of this outcrop there are several red cedars (*Juniperus communis*). The heartwood is aromatic with a rose-brown color. As the wood is light, strong, and durable, it finds use for cedar chests, cabinets, lead pencils, fuel, shingles, and fence posts. When stripped from the tree and rubbed between the hands, the dry outer bark makes an excellent tinder for flint-and-steel or lens fire starts. The oil from the leaves is used in perfumes and polishes. The berries are used to prepare a flavoring.

About a 100 feet down the slope, a large glacial erratic lies to the right of our path. The ground cover is initially early low blueberry (*Vaccinium augustifolium*). Further on the ground cover includes pipsissewa or prince's pine (*Chimaphila umbellata*), a member of the wintergreen family. It blooms about the Fourth of July. Its seed heads persist throughout the winter, often until new bloom occurs. The canopy trees are a mixture of oaks and white pines After passing a small area of hemlock, there is an area containing maple-leaved viburnum (*Viburnum acerifolium*). After passing through a stone wall, we reach the Weston Aqueduct. This aqueduct was built at the turn of the century to connect Wachusett Reservoir to the Boston Water System. In 1994, the aqueduct still carried 15 % of the water distributed by the MWRA system. This gravity aqueduct has since been phased out. When the aqueduct was built, a hand laborer was paid 50 cents a day and a laborer with a horse was paid 5 dollars a day.

The open area to our right is the Pine Brook Golf Club. Go to your right along the aqueduct for 20 feet and turn left into the pines. We enter a hemlock grove. As we pass a dry area, note the vegetation change, and descend into the hemlocks surrounding Hemlock Pond. At the trail junction, bear to your right. After going 25 feet, to your left you will see a shrub that dominates the growth about the edge of the pond. This shrub is sweet pepperbush (*Clethra alnifolia*). It blossoms in July and its flowers may persist until September. These flowers are racemes of small, white blossoms that have a heavy, sweet fragrance. The racemes mature from the bottom up with a few new blossoms opening each day (Figure 12). Initially the petals open only slightly, with the anthers just projecting, so that any insect visiting such a flower picks up pollen as it searches for the nectar. The pistil then elongates beyond the anthers and becomes receptive by opening at its tip. Soon the stamens wither and drop off with the petals leaving only the pistil. Thus, the flower is said to be proterandrous that means that the flower is male and then female. Since the raceme blooms from the bottom up, the flowers at the bottom of a raceme will become female as the male flowers are beginning to open at the top of a raceme. The habit of most bees is to land at the bottom of a raceme and crawl upward. Thus, as a bee leaves from the top of a raceme, the bee has just been loaded with pollen from the male flowers which it carries to the bottom of the next raceme there most of the flowers are in the female stage which assures that the pollen comes from a different raceme.

Fig 12

Another interesting aspect of pepperbush's development is that the flowers of the blooming spike point outward in all directions so that the greatest amount of access is provided to visiting insects. Once fertilized, the maturing fruits turn upward and form small cups to hold the seeds. Shaking of the cup by passing animals or by wind gradually empties the seeds from the cup into the environs.

Crossing a bridge over a tributary to Pine Brook, you will reach the view spot overlooking Hemlock Pond. Note that the trees immediately surrounding Hemlock Pond are mainly red maple, white birch, and yellow birch. Back from the pond are the encircling hemlocks. Go along the path about 100 feet to a junction. Here a plaque on a boulder reads:

> Hemlock Pond Wildlife
> Sanctuary
> in memory of
> Agnes Blake Fitzgerald
> who loved this pond
> and left it for others to enjoy
> Massachusetts Audubon
> Sanctuary
> 1965.

Agnes Blake Fitzgerald (Mrs. Stephen Fitzgerald) lived her life in the southeast corner of Weston and was an original member of the Town Planning Board. Hemlock Pond was one of the several neighborhood ponds where children of this area learned to swim. (Many of the other ponds are now buried under the turnpike.) One afternoon, say in 1958, Dr. William Elliston took two children to the pond for a swim. One of the children suddenly said, oh look, jellyfish. As Bill Elliston had just read a letter that morning in the Herald stating that a rare freshwater jellyfish had been discovered on the Cape, he was immediately able to identify the jellyfish as *Craspedacusta sowerbyi*. One of the jellyfish was taken to the school that day and eventually even appeared on television. Mrs. Fitzgerald felt that this event vindicated her efforts to preserve the natural aspects of Hemlock Pond. It was suggested to her that this attractive pond should be preserved for the future. She accepted this suggestion very graciously and left the area by bequest to the Massachusetts Audubon Society. Later, after the Commonwealth had passed legislation enabling the Town to establish the Conservation Commission, the Conservation Commission approached the Massachusetts Audubon Society as the Society had a policy of transferring small areas into proper hands. Thus, Hemlock Pond became part of the Town Conservation Land in 1979.

Erdna Rogers who lives next to this pond verified that this jellyfish was once present in the pond. She and her children first noticed the quarter-sized jellyfish in the 1940's. They were identified at that time. Erdna feels that the jellyfish are no longer present in the pond either due to its loss of isolation with development of the surrounding area or due to acid rain.

If you turn right at this boulder, you will quickly come to Young Road. We will turn to our left and continue along a woods road through the hemlocks. As the road rises from the moist pond area onto drier, higher land, the understory has many American chestnut suckers. The canopy is largely red oaks and white pine. Also, spruce are found here.

To find an American chestnut, you should look for a sapling with shrubby habit of growth and with long lanceolate leaves that are coarsely toothed (Figure 13). In the autumn, these leaves turn to a distinctive golden brown. These saplings are the stump sprouts of the American chestnut (*Castanea dentata*). At one time, the American chestnut, a member of the beech family, was a common forest species of the Northeast and the

Fig 13

Appalachian region. It was highly prized as an excellent shade tree and for its rot resistant wood that was used for timber frame construction, house siding and shingles, and fencing. Its fruit was an important source of food for wild animals, for roaming farm hogs and for farm families.

In 1904, the American chestnuts close to New York's Bronx Zoo suddenly died revealing the effect of a plant disease that probably came from the Far East. This fungus disease is known as chestnut blight. Most chestnut trees native to the Far East have adapted to this fungus; but the American species that evolved in isolation from the fungus was defenseless. In the next 50 years, the plague spread over the range of the American chestnut. Curiously, the fungus kills the cambium layer (the zone of growth in plants) and sapwood of the trunk without affecting the roots. As a result, American chestnuts that have been killed to the ground continue to produce leaf-bearing suckers. These suckers grow for about ten years before being overwhelmed by the blight. As you walk through Eastern woodlands, you often can observe these suckers amoung the understory plants. Considerable effort has been expended to develop a disease resistant hybrid without a great deal of success to date.

By a highbush blueberry, turn to your right on a footpath leaving the woods road. After about 30 feet, turn left and continue up the slope where there is an open woodland composed largely of red pine. Red pine (*Pinus resinosa*), a native of North America, is sometimes called Norway pine. Red pine cones are small, 1.5" to 2.5", the needles are in clusters of two, and the bark is reddish plates. White pine cones are long and narrow, 3" to 10", the needles are in clusters of five and usually blue-green; while the bark is dark and deeply furrowed. Much of the ground cover here is striped pipsissewa or striped wintergreen (*Chimaphilia maculata*). This area is a bedrock outcrop that separates two drainages. The path drops down through a grove of hemlock and spruce, terminating on a path that runs parallel to a stone wall and an intermittent stream. It is easy to distinguish a hemlock from a spruce. Note that hemlocks have short, flat needles that are darker above and silvery underneath. Hemlock needles lie in two flat rows on either side of the stem. On the other hand, the various spruces have four-sided needles which are nearly square in cross-section and end in sharp points. Spruce needles are arranged in compact spirals around the stem.

Turn to your left and cross a small intermittent stream (usually dry except after a rain or during spring melt) keeping right as you pass through a deciduous area and then through hemlocks. The next small stream is crossed on a bridge. After crossing the bridge, turn to your left paralleling the stream with the hemlock grove on its other side. You will come to a rock outcrop with a bench. Sit for a moment and observe. You will note along the stream there are northern white cedar or Arbor Vitae (*Thuja occidentalis*). White cedar favors moist or swampy soil and its short, light green, scale-like leaves are flattened into fan-like sprays. The shrub along the stream is spicebush. Spicebush (*Lindera benzoin*) is one of the earliest fragrant flowered shrubs to bloom in spring. The yellow blossoms appear in tight little clusters on the bare twigs long before the leaves appear. The flowers are unisexual and the sexes occur on separate plants. The flowers have no petals but have six yellow sepals and a spicy fragrance. In early spring, spicebush's blossoms can be so plentiful that many moist areas display a light yellow haze. Behind the bench, American chestnut suckers may be present.

The plaque on the rock reads:

> William Elliston Woods
> Dedicated in recognition
> of his contributions to
> the conservation efforts
> of the Forest and Trail
> Association
> and to the
> Town of Weston
> May 1978

William A. Elliston was one of the founders of the Forest and Trail Association and served as a Trustee for 30 years. He also served on the Planning Board and as a Conservation Commissioner during most of this period. A fuller description of his life may be requested at the reference desk of the Weston Public Library.

On the top of the rock bearing the plaque is one of the evergreen ferns that are found in our state. It is known as polypody. The French Canadians call it tripe de roche, referring to its habit of growing over rocky surfaces with very shallow soil. In the mountains, it is often found growing at any altitude. In Weston, it can be found on the bedrock outcrops on many hilltops. Continue along the path, pausing to note the pond (may be a muddy spot in late summer and fall) which may be a breeding place for wood frogs and salamanders.

During the summer of 1997, warning signs were erected by the Massachusetts Water Resources Authority (MWRA) along the eastern border of Town Land near the site of construction of an MWRA tank. Construction of this tank may be complete by 2001. The signs warn of blasting in this area and read:

> DANGER
> YOU ARE APPROACHING A
> BLASTING AREA
> PLEASE LEAVE THE AREA
> WHEN YOU HEAR THE
> FOLLOWING
> BLAST WARNING SIGNALS
> 3 - LONG WHISTLES - 5 MINUTES TO BLAST
> 5 - SHORT WHISTLES- 1 MINUTES TO BLAST
> 1 - LONG WHISTLE- ALL CLEAR

These signs may remain in place until about 2001.

The path bears to the right and leaves the stream valley and then ends at another path. Take this path to the left, descending into the hemlocks at the north end of the pool and south of a small swamp. Cross the brook here and ascend the slope into an oak wood. The aqueduct comes into view ahead and we'll climb onto it.

Cross the aqueduct and immediately enter the red oak and hickory woods at the F&T sign.

Fig 14

Between the aqueduct and junction S, you should look for understory shrubs that have leaves which occur in three patterns - unlobed, a "thumb and a mitten", and "three fingers" (Figure 14). This is *Sassafras albidum*, a member of the laurel family. It was highly prized by early English explorers who believed that it had remarkable powers. Sassafras tea was taken to arrest the aging process and many noxious diseases. Wood boxes were made to protect Bibles from the minions of Satan. Sassafras timbers were incorporated into the hulls of seagoing vessels to preserve them from shipwreck. Thoreau observed that "The green leaves have the fragrance of lemons and a thousand spices." This observation applies to the stems and wood. Alas, scientific study of the plant has shown that the principal component of its oil is safrole, a carcinogen.

The path continues gently uphill, soon reaching junction **S**. Turn to your left, go about 100 feet and turn right to continue up the hill. Many interesting plants can be found along the path. The woods become more open as we ascend to reach a view point looking toward Boston. On a sunny afternoon, one may see the gleam of gold leaf on the State House Dome. Just to the right of the four stacks of a power station, one can see the Mystic River Bridge. Then, from the higher rock to your left, you can see the top of Great Blue Hill and its ski slope.

Continuing straight along the ridge, pass the path descending to the right to reach the east summit of Doublet Hill. On the summit rocks, there usually is a fine display of *Corydalis sempervirens* that is known under many names. My favorite name is Rock Harlequin that hints where it is found and that its flowers are pink and yellow. Some other common names are Pale or Pink Corydalis. In dry years, it blooms during June; in wet years, it blooms from June to the first heavy frost.

Underneath the corydalis, one may find dwarf dandelion (*Krigia virginica*). Unlike the dandelions that grow on lawns and which are European plants, the dwarf dandelion is a native plant that is closely related to the hawkweeds. This plant blooms most heavily at the end of May and then sporadically through the summer.

The path now descends to the area near the water tank where this walk began and your car should be in view.

HUBBARD TRAIL
AND
VICINITY

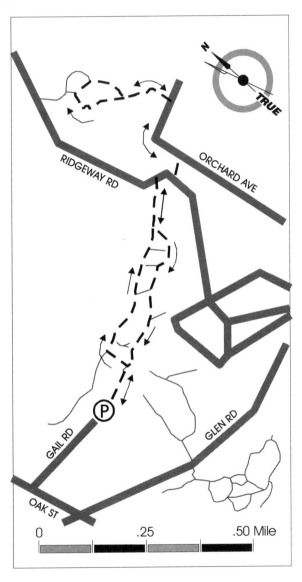

MAP 7

GENERAL INFORMATION:
In the southeast corner of Weston, there are several parcels of land which were portions of the Charles W. Hubbard estate. The Hubbard Trail of the Forest & Trail Association has an area of 24 acres. To the east between Ridgeway Road and Orchard Avenue is a 1.76 acre field given to the Forest & Trail Association by Stanley G. French. North of Orchard Avenue and running west to Ridgeway Road is a parcel of 4.68 acres belonging to the Forest & Trail Association next to 13.5 acres of Town Conservation land. The Town Recreation Department has a ball field at the end of Gail Road lying to the south of the Hubbard Trail. Originally, this ball field was known as "Jennings Field" as it was taken from the Jennings' Glen Farm in lieu of taxes during the 1930's. It was renamed Burt Field in 1982.

PARKING:
The parking lot at the end of Gail Road gives convenient access to this area.

RECOMMENDED WALK:
Beginning at the Gail Road parking lot, walk to the ball field. At the right field foul line, there is a boulder bearing a plaque which reads:

> ED BURT
> 1924 — 1980
> MEMORIAL FIELD
> DEDICATED
> MAY 31, 1982

Roger   Sperber,   a   former   Recreation
Commissioner, said that Ed Burt was involved
in Little League Baseball as a coach and as a
general manager. He was a tireless volunteer for
Little League and was devoted to improving the
quality of the Little League experience for the
children of Weston.

Continue along the right foul line to the
backstop. Turn right along the left foul line to
the corner of left field. A trail enters the woods
by some cedars and immediately passes through
a stone wall. In about 10 feet, you are at a
gateway in an old fence. Turn left and pass
through the gateway keeping to your left along
a wide trail. During the spring and summer, one
can find bracken (*Pteridium aquilinum*), the
commonest of the ferns, hairy Solomon's seal
(*Polygonatum pubescens*), and wild spikenard
(*Smilacina racemosa*) in this area. The area also
has escaped lily-of-the-valley and wild lily-of-
the-valley or Canada mayflower (*Maianthemum
canadense*). The trail soon reaches a junction. On
the left, the path goes to Oak Street. However,
you should go right along the Hubbard Trail
that follows Hubbard Brook to Ridgeway Road.
The trail descends to and crosses Hubbard
Brook. Just after crossing the brook there is a
hemlock grove on the left and a wetland to your
right. Here one can find New York fern
(*Thelypteris noveboracensis*) which is abundant in
semimoist regions. The large wetland ferns are
cinnamon   fern   (*Osmunda   cinnamomea*),
interrupted fern (*Osmunda claytoniana*), royal

fern (*Osmunda regalis*) and ostrich fern (*Matteuccia struthiopteriis*). The osmunda family originated in the final part of the Paleozoic era - 250 million years before the present. At present, these ancient spore producing plants are more

prevalent and successful than at any other time in their history. Throughout this area, one may also find wild geraniums or cranesbills (*Geranium* sp.) (Figure 15). Note, that the valley has the typical "U" shaped profile of a mature valley

Fig 15

Fig 16

The wood soon opens out into a mixed woodland with white pine and oaks predominating on the drier slope. Keep on the main trail avoiding the trails leading across the valley to your right. About 1950, several townsmen planted a selection of spring wildflowers in this valley. However, the area has not been maintained and little of this garden remains. In about 10 to 15 minutes, you will reach an old reservoir. In the wet land beyond the dam, one may find lesser celandine (*Ranunculus ficaria*) with its buttercup-like flowers. In drier areas, there is spring beauty (*Claytonia virginica*) (Figure 16) and some trilliums.

This reservoir belonged to a water company owned by Charles W. Hubbard. His water company was one of at least five water companies that served local neighborhoods during the late nineteenth and early twentieth century until the Town Water Department was established. Beyond the reservoir, you reach Ridgeway Road. Cross the road and turn to your right. Follow along the road until you come to the end of the line of concrete highway posts. Turn to your left crossing the field while heading for the yellow fire hydrant on Orchard Avenue. This field was given to the Town by Stanley G. French, one of the original trustees of the Forest & Trail Association. Turn left on Orchard Avenue, cross the brook, and either follow the road around the curve or turn to your right and follow a mowed path through a meadow.

Either route brings you to a road bump alongside a hedge. Turn to your left through the opening in the hedge beside the road bump. Follow the mowed trail up the slope. Just before the trail begins to descend, you should turn left into the woods and follow a trail. The fenced mound on your left is another of the Hubbard reservoirs. If you turn to your left just as you reach the reservoir and walk to where there is a stone stairway leading up the side of the reservior. You can peer into the reservior where you can see a dedication stone that reads:

BUILT BY FRANCIS BLAKE
-1880-
ENGINEER
C. H. M. BLAKE.
SUPERINTENDENT
O.P. MURDOCK.

Water was pumped into this tank from what is now the ninth hole on the MDC golf course. This reservoir is situated at the top of a small drumlin. A drumlin is a streamlined hill of glacial till, a non stratified sediment of varying particle size (clay to boulders). The long dimension of a drumlin parallels the direction of ice flow.

Return to the trail and continue straight along the ridge disregarding the trail going to your right. On the forest floor in this mixed woodland, two members of the wintergreen family are common - striped or spotted wintergreen (*Chimaphila maculata*) (Figure 17) and pipsissewa or prince's pine (*Chimaphila umbellata*) (Figure 18). Both of these plants bloom in early July and are members of the wintergreen family. When the trail drops down from the drumlin, you should keep right as we are making a loop and heading back to the reservoir. Head up the slope on a narrow, steep

Fig 17

trail just before reaching a house. At the top of the slope, you will again be by the reservoir

From here, you will retrace your steps - out to the meadow, turning right and following the meadow path to Orchard Avenue, turning right on Orchard Avenue and going around the curve to the yellow hydrant opposite 140 Orchard Avenue, crossing the meadow to Ridgeway Road, turning right again and going to

Fig 18

the yellow fire hydrant across from 136 Ridgeway Road. Turn left onto the Hubbard Trail once again. Just beyond the reservoir, follow the trail to your left. Once on this trail, note the large rock mass to your left. It is a bedrock outcrop. You will soon cross the stream again. Avoid the trail going to the right. You will follow along the stream for some time. Note that in some places the stream has been dug out and the trail is situated along the top of the spoil.

The path reaches a wide trail going left to Dean Road. At this point bear right crossing a culvert and walking through a wetland. Take the first trail on your left which heads uphill. This trail soon reaches the gap in an old fence. Just beyond is the ball field from which we started.

COLD STREAM
BROOK

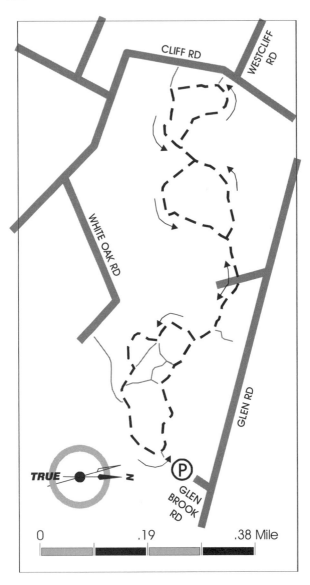

MAP 8

GENERAL INFORMATION:
Cold Stream Brook (Glen Brook) arises in Weston and flows to Wights Pond in Wellesley. Access along the brook is provided by 14.5 acres of Weston Conservation land, several easements, by land belonging to the Wellesley Conservation Council and the 10.5 acre Carisbrooke Reservation of the Wellesley Conservation Commission.

A short history of this land is: William Jennison from Colchester, England came with John Winthrop and settled in Watertown in 1630. He was granted several tracts of land in Watertown. In 1642, he received a grant of 150 acres of farm land sited in this area. He returned to Colchester in 1645 where he spent the remainder of his life. This Watertown farm land grant was on the Dedham line. Weston was formed from the western part of Watertown in 1713. The northerly part of Dedham became Needham in 1711 and then Wellesley in 1881. So today, the 1642 grant is now on the Wellesley/Weston boundary.

About 1732, Nathaniel Jennison, the nephew thrice removed of William Jennison, moved to the Weston land grant and built the house which is now sited at 266 Glen Road. This house is now occupied by George P. Bates who is the second cousin seven times removed of Nathaniel Jennison.

PARKING:
One may park at the end of Glen Brook Road
that is on right side of Glen Road immediately
south of the Weston/Wellesley Line as you
enter Wellesley from Weston.

RECOMMENDED WALK:
A sign marks the parking lot at the end of Glen
Brook Road. The sign reads:

```
CARISBROOK
RESERVATION
Town of Wellesley
```

Just beyond and slightly to the left of this sign,
there is a large granite stone which reads:

```
Joseph Covati Brook
Town of Wellesley
Designed by Joseph Covati
Assistant Town Engineer
1959 – 1987
We thank him for restoring the vigor and
sound of running water to Carisbrook Reservation
NATURAL RESOURCES    PUBLIC WORKS
```

Go to your right from the sign and continue
across a culvert. About 100 feet beyond the
culvert, you will note a salmon colored area of
bedrock on your right. This granite is an
example of the oldest rock in this area being late

Precambrian. As this granite was first described from a formation in Dedham, it is known as Dedham Granite. In 1982, its age was determined to be 605 to 610 million years. The large salmon colored crystals are a potassium feldspar containing a trace of iron giving the granite its color. Rocks south of the railroad tracks in Wellesley are younger and are an extension of the Boston Basin sediments and volcanics. In May, our native wild columbine (*Aquilegia canadensis*) with its showy red and yellow flowers may be found growing here and on other ledgy spots in the area.

The trail goes uphill, levels out, and then crosses a wooden bridge over the brook. Just beyond the bridge, take the first trail to your right. As you enter this trail you will note on your right a winged euonymus (*Euonymus alatus*). This introduced shrub is common along the trails in this area. It is readily recognized by its four-sided stems which have thin, bladelike, corky ridges on the four sides. Often on the older stems, the corky material may be broken off and the ridges may be less prominent. It is the only shrub in eastern North America which displays these ridges. The chief attraction of this Asian species is its stunning fall foliage which is a translucent pink. Its fruits are red and enclosed in a purple capsule. The appearance of the fruit betrays the fact that euonymus is a member of the same plant family as bittersweet. Like bittersweet, winged euonymus is an invasive plant.

Carefully observe the rock outcrops in this area. The first outcrop is covered with haircap moss and with the fern, common polypody (*Polypodium vulgare*) (Figure 19), which is evergreen and tends to form a mantle-like growth on rocky surfaces. The second outcrop displays two evergreen ferns - common

Fig 19

polypody and evergreen, leatherleaf, or marginal woodfern (*Dryoptersis marginalis*) (Figure 20). If you examine a leaf of marginal woodfern, you will note that the fruit dots are formed along the edges or margins of the leaves in the late summer and persist throughout the year. The trail now drops down into a wash and then climbs again. Along the trail here, Christmas fern (*Polystichum acrostichoides*) (Figure 21) can be found. The leaflets of this fern resemble old fashioned knee high stockings.

Fig 20

The Wellesley Guide refers to this area, north of the Carisbrooke Reservation, which lies in Weston as The George L. Lienau Memorial Trail. George L. Lienau was an active member of the Wellesley Conservation Council and an original member of the Wellesley Conservation Commission. He was a past president of the Boston Camera Club and an outstanding photographer.

Keep to your right at the junction. Soon you can see the houses along Glen Road (Weston) and will come to a junction behind a yellow house. This yellow house was built by Nathaniel Jennison about 1732. In the early 1900's, there was a small water system here which served 32 houses along Glen Road. The Glen Farm Water Company pumped water using a windmill from a well behind 266 Glen Road and at a second site further east.

At the junction, continue straight ahead and along the side of a meadow (lawn) on an

Fig 21

easement, marked by concrete boundary stones at your left side. Cross Summit Road and enter Forest & Trail land keeping the pond to your right. Pass through a stone wall where there is a junction. Keep right on the trail that enters an area with old cedars and young white pines. The trail soon drops down and crosses an intermittent stream. Further on, we pass through a stone wall. At a junction about 20 feet beyond the wall, keep to your right. At the next junction, again bear right, cross a bridge, and enter a small hemlock grove. Just ahead a bedrock outcrop overlooks a marsh to the left. To the right is a small pond. The trail drops down into a small wetland before rising again to where Cliff Road can be seen. Bear to the left entering a grove of 30 to 40 year old hemlocks. The trail parallels Cliff Road for a short time.

Soon you cross a bridge. The trail leaves the hemlocks bearing left and away from Cliff Road. The trail soon rises to the top of a higher area and passes through a stone wall onto an old road that parallels the wall for a short distance. Keeping to the right, you will arrive at a trail junction marked by F & T signs, bear right. At the top of the ridge, we head back to Summit Road, making a semicircle by keeping to the left. Note the orange to salmon bed rock outcrops in this region of the woods. These are outcrops of Dedham Granite.

After crossing Summit Road, retrace your steps along the edge of the meadow (lawn). Behind the yellow house, the trail is covered with wood chips. On your left, just after the wood chips end, there is a group of nine similar trees. These trees are recognized by having a rough dark outer bark with horizontal lines formed by cracking of the bark. The cracks are sometimes reddish-brown as are the smaller twigs. These trees are black cherry (*Prunus serotina*), a common New England tree, and are one of the largest cherries. It is important as a food source and for lumber. The fruit is red changing to black. It has a bitter-sweet and wine-like flavor and is often used to make jelly and wine. Its bark has been used as a flavoring. The fruit is also eaten by many songbirds, ruffed grouse, pheasant, raccoon, black bear, red fox, whitetail deer, cottontail rabbit, and gray squirrel. It's heavy, warp-resistant wood polishes to a deep and luminous red tone. It has been a favorite material for tabletops, cabinets, and paneling, and even U.S. dollar-bill plates. The wood is sometimes known as "Connecticut mahogany". In October, its green leaves turn yellow to brilliant wine-red. It can be a pest in a yard as black cherries tend to be weedy.

Almost opposite the black cherry trees, there is a shrub or small tree that is very showy in the fall. This is the European spindletree (*Euonymus europaeus*). Its fruit resembles that of bittersweet having pink to red capsule that opens to display four orange to red seeds. This tree is short lived in this location.

Just beyond the black cherries and next to the European spindletree, you should turn to the right on a trail that crosses a wetland and slowly climbs to a ridge. Follow along the ridge as the trail meanders. A stone wall soon parallels the trail. Beyond the wall, there is a vernal pond. This stone wall was once considered to divide Wellesley from Weston and to divide Middlesex and Norfolk counties. The actual boundary is to the southeast of the stone wall. Cross the wall and take the trail going to the right. This trail enters Wellesley and meanders up and down. Where the trail curves around the vernal pool, you can see a large glacial erratic in the pool. Right along the trail in this area, there is a bed rock outcrop. Note the polypody growing here. Closer to the trail, there can be found hair cap moss.

The trail turns back on itself as passes behind some houses. Keep to the right at the next two intersections. The path descends to a wet area. The trail going to the right goes out to White Oak Road in Wellesley. Avoid this trail and keep going straight ahead. Soon, you will cross a bridge. Just beyond this bridge you will be able to see the houses at the end of Glen Brook Road where we started.

WALK

THE BLANEY
AQUIFER

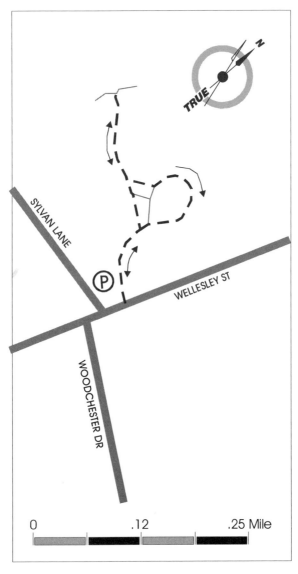

MAP 9

GENERAL INFORMATION:
The Blaney aquifer serves as a water recharge area for the water supply of the Town of Wellesley. Nonesuch Brook rises in this area and flows to Nonesuch Pond. This pond empties into Bogle Brook. This brook flows into Morse Pond and then into Lake Waban that empties via Waban Brook into the Charles River just south of Wellesley College. Some of this area is situated in an outwash plain of glacial Lake Sudbury (see Chapter 10). The total area of the Conservation land is about 65 acres. Most of the land is an extensive wetland.

PARKING:
Park on Sylvan Lane just off Wellesley Street.

RECOMMENDED WALK:
This is a short walk which requires about a half hour. From the corner of Sylvan Lane and Wellesley Street, walk north on the sidewalk along Wellesley Street for about 150 feet. On the left is a gate. Pass around the gate and walk along the south edge of the meadow. Once you have passed a fenced garden on the right, you should head for the solitary oak standing in the meadow which is marked with Forest & Trail signs.

Continue west from the oak, avoiding the trails leading to your right, to a group of cedars at the woodland edge. Enter the woods and walk over a small hummock. The wood is largely red and black oak with white pines. Drop down off the hummock into a short stretch of sphagnum bog. You may see deer tracks in the soft mud of this bog.The most common fern in this wetland is the cinnamon fern (*Osmunda cinnamomea*) (Figure 4). Soon, the trail regains higher land. The iron pipes to the right of the trail are test wells placed by the Weston Water Department in their attempt to find a water supply after Weston's Nickerson well had been contaminated by the salting of the Massachusetts Turnpike Authority toll booth plazas which are situated just above the well that was the main supply of town water. The trail ends at an upside down Forest & Trail arrow. Retrace your steps just about to the cedars at the end of the meadow.

Fig 4

Just before reaching the meadow, there is a loop trail to the left which passes through a white pine woods. When you exit the woods, you can see the oak in the meadow in front of you. Retrace your steps to your car.

ASH STREET
CONSERVATION LANDS

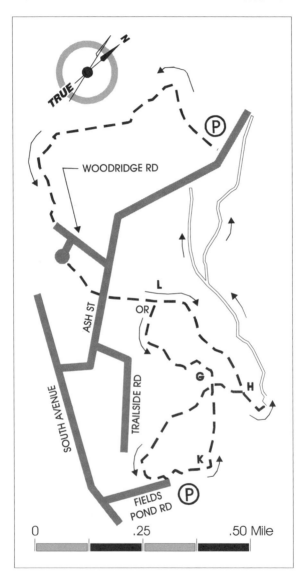

MAP 10

GENERAL INFORMATION:

The Weston Reservoir was completed in 1900 to serve Boston. At present, the Weston Reservior is managed by the Metropolitan Water Resources Authority. The reservoir and its supply system do not meet present day standards and were phased out in 1995. South of the reservoir, the Town of Weston owns 53 acres of conservation land. An additional parcel of 7 acres was given to the Forest and Trail Association by Leon Cohen. These parcels are connected by trail easements granted to the Weston Forest & Trail Association. Most of the area is forested with hickory, oak, and white pine.

PARKING:

The most convenient parking spot is on the west side of Ash Street just south of the reservoir.

RECOMMENDED WALK:

This walk will focus on the geology of this area and requires about 1 to 2 hours depending upon route selection.

Start from the south end of the parking lot on the west side of Ash Street and walk about 200 feet south. By a drainage ditch on the right, there is a large white pine marked with a Forest & Trail sign. Cross the ditch on a pair of railroad ties and continue west along a trail. Note that many of the white pines are about a yard in diameter. I assume that during the 1938 hurricane these trees were protected by their location in this valley enclosed on the south and west. Poison ivy vines form the ground cover here and run up the pines held by aerial roots. Be careful! Eventually, you will pass through a stone wall. Look to your left and note a pond that lies in a depression with a 50 foot bluff on its south side. I believe that this pond is a kettle hole pond. A kettle hole results when a buried block of glacial ice melts away, leaving a depression. If water fills this depression, it is referred to as a kettle hole lake or pond. The ice block that formed this kettle rested against the bluff that was a part of the southerly shore of glacial Lake Sudbury.

About 50 feet beyond the wall, the trail climbs an irregular mound and meanders as it heads to the south. This mound is an example of an esker, a glacial deposit that is a continually winding ridge formed from the deposits of a stream which once flowed within a glacier.

Upon reaching the top of the bluff, the former southern shore of the glacial Lake Sudbury, the trail runs along a stone wall that approximates the course of an outlet of glacial Lake Sudbury. At first, the trail runs along the right side of the stone wall. Then, by a house, the trail passes through the wall and runs along with the wall on your right. After passing behind four houses on your left, the trail meets a crossing trail. The outflow from the glacial Lake Sudbury flowed to the south forming an outwash plain. The outwash plain extends toward the southwest to

Nonesuch Pond. The high school athletic fields, the high school, and junior high school are built on this outwash plain.

The trail to the right goes to Wellesley Street. However, you should turn up hill to your left. The trail ends on another trail by a small mountain laurel (*Kalmia latifolia*) thicket. Mountain laurel, a common plant of our woodlands, grows about 3 to 7 feet in height in Weston and may bloom from mid-June through mid-July. Continue straight ahead through the hickory/oak forest. Take a left at the next junction. The small laurel plants, ranging from 0.5 to 3 feet high along the trail are sheep laurel or lambkill (*Kalmia angustifolia*) which may bloom in June. The name, lambkill, reminds us that many of our native laurels and rhododendrons are toxic to many of the grazing animals introduced from the Old World. However, our native white-tail deer feed on our native laurels and rhododendrons with relish much to the despair of gardeners.

The trail emerges from the woods at the end of Woodridge Road. One may take either of two routes from here for the continuation of this walk. One may simply follow Woodridge Road out to Ash Street, cross to the sidewalk on the east side, and walk south just beyond 47 Ash Street to the third post on the fence along the Ash Street sidewalk.

The other way is to follow Woodridge Road to the first intersection on the right. Turn down Woodridge Circle. At the telephone pole north of number 12 Woodridge Circle, there should be a Forest & Trail arrow indicating a trail which leads east through the woods. Start from the pole with the wooden fence to your left. At the end of the fence, the trail route is clear and emerges between number 40 and 48 Ash Street. Cross Ash Street to the side walk, turn left along the fence, and walk to the <u>third</u> <u>post</u> from the north end of the fence.

Looking into the woods from this post you should see a Forest & Trail arrow along a trail leading back into the woods. As you reenter Conservation land, the trail goes through a wetland. In the spring, the wetland may be a pool and you may have to bushwhack around it. Just beyond the wetland, the trail rises. Here is junction **L**. Again, one may take either of two routes. The shorter route goes straight ahead and down a slope to junction **H**. The slope is the bluff that once was a southern shore of glacial Lake Sudbury. If you follow this shorter route, skip the next four paragraphs.

To take either of the longer routes to junction **H**, turn to your right and follow the trail which remains on the top of the ridge. There are many bedrock outcrops and small wetlands along this trail. At junction **F**, bear slightly to your left. The trail going right continues to Trailside Road. Ignore the next junction (no label) and continue straight along the trail to junction **E**. At junction **E**, continue straight avoiding the trail to the right (this trail is very soggy). The trail drops down into the valley of a small, intermittent stream, crosses the steam, and rises again. Avoid the trails to your left (these return to junction **E**), when you reach a trail junction by a stone wall, you are at junction **G**. Here you may take either of two routes. The first and shorter route continues straight ahead and follows the stone wall down to junction **H**. If you follow this route, skip the next three paragraphs.

To take the longest route, pass through the stone wall at junction **G** and immediately turn to your right. Continue about 100 feet and pass through another stone wall. About twenty feet beyond this stone wall, you should turn to your left. As you follow this trail, you may note that, on your left, there is either a stone wall or rock outcrops and on your right, there is a a wetland. Soon, the trail turns away from the wall and skirts the wetland. Watch for deer tracks in the moist spots in the trail. Behind a house at the end of Trailside Road, there are several short stretches of corduroy through moist spots. Here, with luck, you may be serenaded by a wood thrush during May and June. At junction **J**, a right turn will bring you to the end of Trailside Road. However, you should turn left onto private land. The owner allows us to use these trails over his land. Please respect his rights to his land. When you reach an old abandoned road, turn left to follow along the abandoned road.

After crossing a wooden bridge, the road reaches the end of Fields Pond Road. Descend to the road and pass through the wooden gate on your left. Continue north along the road until you see a pair of stone gate posts on your left. These posts are at junction **K**.

Take the path to your left and pass between the posts. Soon, the trail passes some old pasture cedars. Fifty feet beyond these is a large rhododendron. Behind this rhododendron are the remains of two old cabins - foundations, a small chimney, metal table, stove parts, bed frames, and a bath tub. Some items, found here, suggest that the cabins were probably last used about 1940. These remains serve to remind us that before 1950, many people summered in Weston.

Continue to the west along the trail which leaves the private land and passes through a stone wall to junction **G**. Take the trail to the right which drops down the slope that formed the southern shore of glacial Lake Sudbury to junction **H**.

From junction **H**, continue to the east for a short distance and then make two left turns to the road running along the fence enclosing the Weston Reservoir. Follow the fence to the west. When you reach a "Y", I suggest that you take the road to the left that passes through an area of cedars and spruce trees. Walking either this way or keeping to the right along the Reservoir fence will return you to the parking lot from which this walk began.

Mushroom
(Family *Polyporaceae* probably Genius *Deadalae*)

Chicken or Sulphurous Mushroom
(*Polyporus sulphurous*)

WALK 11

PINE STREET
TOWN
FOREST

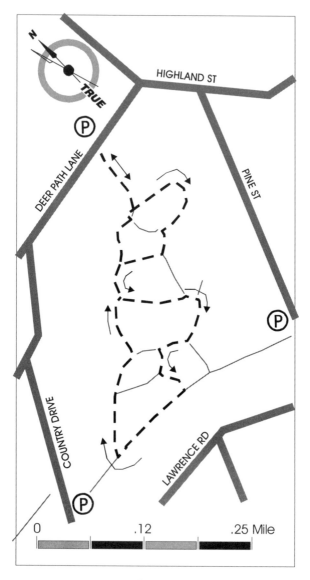

MAP 11

GENERAL INFORMATION:

The Pine Street Town Forest with an area of 21 acres was at the southern end of the Dickson Estate. Brenton H. Dickson, Jr. bought the land from a farmer, Lemuel Smith. The highest point, called Mount Lemuel by the Dickson family, lies at 356 feet above sea level and was the site of a cabin used by Anna Dickson Ela. This cabin was built by a Vermont craftsman in about 1930. Anna would invite Girl Scouts from the Ellis Memorial, a Boston settlement house, who would camp in tents in the area about the cabin. In 1977, this area was named "The Stanley French Conservation Area" in honor of Mr. French, long-time chairman of the Conservation Commission, Planning Board member, Trustee of the Weston Forest and Trail Association, and driving force in our conservation acquisition program.

PARKING:

There are three entrances to this area:

1) From Deer Path Lane: Head south between 12 and 24 Deer Path Lane along the eastern leg of the "U" drive from 24 Deer Path Lane. The Forest & Trail signs can be seen slightly to the left as you leave the street. The path soon passes through a stone wall and enters into Town Conservation Land.

2) From Pine Street: Just north of the driveway to 55 Pine Street, there is a

stone wall. Head into the woods keeping the stone wall to your left. You should soon see the Forest & Trail signs in front of you.

3) From Country Drive: Just north of the junction of Lawrence Road and Country Drive and before reaching the driveway of 221 Country Drive, there is a stone wall. Head east into the woods keeping the stone wall to your left. You should soon see the Forest & Trail signs in front of you.

RECOMMENDED WALK:

Start from eastern leg of the "U" drive from 24 Deer Path Lane. The Forest & Trail signs can be seen slightly to the left as you leave the street. The path soon passes through a stone wall and enters into Town Conservation Land.

Sixty feet beyond the wall, there is a trail junction. Take the path going to the left that drops into a valley. The upper part of the slope is covered with pipsissewa or prince's pine (*Chimaphila umbellata*) Figure 18) which is recognized by its whorls of dark green shiny evergreen leaves. This plant, a member of the wintergreen family, is common throughout Weston and blooms in July.

Lower down on the bank, there are several types of plants about six inches high which resemble small Christmas trees. These plants, which are common in our less disturbed woodlands, are primitive members of the plant kingdom. They are commonly known as club mosses, ground pines, (Figure 22) or ground cedars. They do resemble tiny conifers but rather than

Fig 22

reproducing by forming seeds like the pine, they reproduce by the earlier method of dispersing spores like the ferns. Members of this family (*Lycopodiaceae*) dominated the coal swamps of the Carboniferous Period (280 to 345 million years ago) when they existed as trees. The organic remains of these trees and their spores are the principal component of coal. The spores of club mosses were a very important item of commerce. They are so minute and uniform in size that they were used in microscopy as measurement standards. These spores are water-repellent and dust-like so they found use in soothing powers for chafes and wounds and as a coating for pills. They were used for fireworks and photographic flashes as they give an explosive flash when ignited. With luck, you may be able to find several different club mosses during this walk.

As the path crosses the valley, it turns south and rises again to an old farm path. Turn right and bear to the left at the next junction. At the next junction, take the path up the slope. As you climb the slope, the large green mats are haircap

mosses.   The path levels out and meets a
crossing path.   Take this new path to the left.
When the path soon splits in two, go to the left
descending along a stream. When the path again
divides, go right. In a 100 feet, the path crosses
the stream that is now underground. In spring
and early summer, there is a display of wild
geranium   or   spotted   cranesbill   (*Geranium
maculatum*) (Figure 15, page 99) in this moist
area. Keep bearing right. When the path next
divides, take the right fork up the hill. At the
next split, go left to the summit of Mount
Lemuel. The summit is a bed rock outcrop. Near
the west side of the summit, you can see the
chimney of Anna Dickson Ela's cabin.

Take the path that goes past the chimney and to
the south.   After passing through two stone
walls, the path intersects the path running
between Pine Street and Country Drive. Go right
on this path. Along the base of the wall that
parallels the path on your right, you many be
able to find striped or spotted wintergreen
(*Chimaphila maculata*) (Figure 17, page 101)
which resembles pipsissewa — blooming in July
but having variegated leaves with a white stripe
along the veins. The plant may have reddish
stems. The path descends, passes through a
stone wall, and soon levels out again. Just where
the path levels out, there is a low spot in the
wall. Turn right passing through the low spot
and again head uphill. The path passes through
a second wall near a large pine. There often is a

squirrel midden on this wall where a squirrel eats its fill of pine seeds.

In about 100 feet, there is a path going to the right. This path returns you to the viewpoint. I suggest that you look along the north side of the ledge on which the path is situated. Here, you should find the fern known as common polypody (*Polypodium vulgare*) (Figure 19, page 108). In Quebec, this fern is known as tripe de roche referring to its rich, lustrous, evergreen growth over rocky surfaces.

Return to the main path that you may have left. Continue on to the north, avoiding any path on your right. When you see a white house to your left, watch carefully for a path to your left. This first path to your left returns you to our starting place.

Spotted Turtle
(*Clemmys guttata*)
A state listed rare species
Resident in Jericho Town Forest

12

HIGHLAND STREET
FOREST

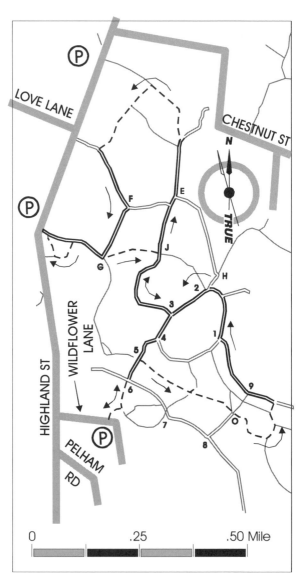

MAP 12

GENERAL INFORMATION:

Sanderson Hill, one of the highest elevations in Weston, is located in the Highland Street Forest. During the American Revolution, this hill was the site of a signal beacon manned by a "Sergeant at the Beacon" and five men. The "Sergeant at the Beacon" was Jonas Sanderson whose house was on Highland Street near the corner of Love Lane. An old photograph of the Sanderson home and barns appeared in *The Weston Historical Society Bulletin*, Vol. IX, No. 2 (January 1973). The house burnt in 1897. Old maps indicate that the beacon was situated near the site of the present water tank. An archaeologist, employed by the Bicentennial Committee, was unable to locate any evidence of the beacon at this site. For a further discussion of the Beacon, see Harold G. Travis, "The Beacon on Sanderson Hill" which appeared in *The Weston Historical Society Bulletin*, Vol. XI, No. 1 (October 1974).

During Weston's estate era (1870 until about 1960), this land was a portion of the estate of General Charles Jackson Paine. General Paine was a grandson of Robert Treat Paine, a signer of the Declaration of Independence. He served throughout the Civil War. After being mustered out of service, he turned his attention to business and took part in the management of several railroads, including the Atchison, Topeka, & Santa Fe and the Chicago, Burlington & Quincy. In 1885, he was a member of a syndicate that built the America's Cup winner,

Puritan. In the two succeeding years, he
assumed the cost of two Cup winners, the
Mayflower and the Volunteer.

General Paine married Julia Bryant in 1867.
Within a year, he bought land in Weston for a
farm. He owned about 700 acres most of which
was located in the area from The Boston Post
Road (Central Avenue) to the Turnpike and
from Highland Street to Wellesley Street. A
further interest of Paine's was trotting horses.
He maintained two race tracks on the farm. The
site of a half-mile track is a part of the Forest &
Trail Association's trail system behind Regis
College (junctions 1, 2, 3, and 4 are on this track).
The Paine family lived on Louisburg Square
during the winter, in Weston during the spring
and fall, and in Nahant or Chatham during the
summer. After General Paine's death, his son
John B. Paine winterized the Weston house and
raised his family there. The house was
abandoned about 1965 and torn down in 1971.

The first land purchased for the Weston Town
Forest was 150 acres of the Paine estate. Since
that time, there have been several additions
including an 18 acre gift of Kenneth J.
Germeshausen and Edward B. Hubbard and a 5
acre gift with Highland Street frontage from the
Paine family. The present area is about 200
acres.

PARKING:

There are three convenient parking spots south of Route 20 along Highland Street.

1) At 0.5 mile south of Route 20, there is a pull-off on the western side of Highland Street After parking, cross Highland Street to the sidewalk and walk south to the telephone pole where the sidewalk ends. About ten feet beyond the telephone pole, there is a path over private land which leads to the meadow at the northwestern end of Highland Street Town Forest.

2) At 1.0 mile south of Route 20, there is a pull-off by a large white pine on the western side of Highland Street at Sunset Corner. After parking, cross Highland Street to a stone staircase which leads to Sunset Corner Lookout on the west side of Highland Street Town Forest.

3) At 1.3 miles south of Route 20 on the east side of Highland Street is Wildflower Lane. Turn into this Lane. On the south side of the Lane is transformer MH 9841 opposite a light colored boulder. Park by the boulder. The walk descrbed below starts from this location.

One may also park on the High School parking lot and walk to the corner of South Avenue (Route 30) and Wellesley Street. Cross to the northwest corner of this intersection. From here one can walk:

1) North along Wellesley Street. Just south of a stone wall behind the Spellman Stamp Museum, turn to your left and pass through a gap in the stone wall to enter a path into the Highland Street Town Forest.

2) West along the north side of South Avenue (Route 30). Just before reaching the Farmer's Cemetery, turn right and follow the path into the hemlock grove. This path is mentioned in the discussion below.

RECOMMENDED WALK:
This walk will start from Wildflower Lane, go down a valley, then to the top of Sanderson Hill before returning to the starting place. The time of this walk is about two hours.

Park by the large light colored boulder on the north side of Wildflower Lane. Enter the woods north of this boulder through a break in the stone wall. Head north along a foot path which runs under a mixture of black oaks, red oaks, red maples, and white pine. Oaks are members of the beech family and belong in either of two groups, the black oaks or the white oaks. Black oaks require two years to form mature acorns, have leaves with sharp lobes with pins at their end, and usually have dark bark. White oaks mature acorns in a single year, have leaves with rounded lobes, and have lighter bark. There are many oak species and many hybrids of these species in New England. To establish identification, one should look at tree form, leaves, buds, bark, and acorns. Oaks are an important source of food for wildlife. In years when the acorn (mast) crop fails, many birds and mammals have difficulty in finding enough to eat during the winter.

After entering the woods, avoid the path leaving on the right and go straight ahead (north) to junction **6**. Continue straight ahead (north) along a fire road. This fire road passes through a stone wall and soon reaches junction **5**. At junction **5**, a foot path crosses the road. Take this path to the right (east). This path rises over a bedrock outcrop and continues down a stream

Fig 23

valley. The path passes through an area of white pine with an understory of bracken or brake. Bracken (*Pteridium aquilinum*) (Figure 23) has three triangular leaves at the top of a stem that is usually higher than a foot. Bracken is native to Africa, North America, Central America, Asia and Europe. For a primitive plant, it has many ways of defending itself. Its stem fibers may inflict deep cuts. Animals attempting to browse on bracken receive not only cuts but a dose of toxic chemicals that destroy reserves of vitamin B, that kill bone marrow and blood cells, and that may cause blindness.

Success of bracken and other ferns illustrates an important point. Long-term survival is not simply a case of being more evolutionary advanced than other forms of life. In each environment on earth, a certain set of factors works to promote survival while other sets fail. Nature refuses to limit its options to man's simplistic idea of evolutionary progress. Ferns using a cumbersome mode of sexual propagation which predates the efficiencies by propagation of seeds, have survived for 300 million years. Very few organisms have had such success. A hot topic in paleontology is the idea that mass extinction has occurred time and time again over geological time. No extinction gets more attention in the media than that of the dinosaurs at the end of the Cretaceous Period. Before and after this extinction, the pollen of the angiosperms, the flowering plants, dominated the fossil record. Nevertheless, during the time of the extinction event, fern spores dominated angiosperm pollen. This fact suggests that ferns were best able to exploit the opportunity provided by the meteor impact, climatic change, or whatever else wiped out so many organisms, including the dinosaurs.

Another more recent example occurred in the gradual transition that resulted from a worldwide cooling during the glacial period that ended ten thousand years ago. The conifers, considered more primitive than the angiosperms, claimed the huge cold area of the earth's surface known as the taiga. Thus, we see that under certain stresses, ferns and conifers have proved more capable of dealing with environmental change than the angiosperms. One may argue that the angiosperms dominate the most favorable climates. But consider a black spruce in a Labrador bog that finds the winters of Labrador to be perfection. To be anthropomorphic, it occupies the best set of conditions; and one can imagine it pitying the poor plants suffering the summer heat and smog of Los Angeles. To repeat, our ideas of primitiveness, success, and dominance are based on our biases more than the way Nature proceeds.

Avoid the trail that crosses our path and continue straight ahead into an area of beeches. Passing through a stone wall, you enter into a hemlock grove. I am told that this grove was completely uprooted during the 1938 hurricane. The windfall was salvaged for timber.

At junction **O**, continue bearing slightly to the right taking a foot path which passes through a stone wall. This path meanders through the hemlock grove trending to the east. You may note that the hemlocks form a dense canopy above you. One result of this dense canopy is that a hemlock grove is cooler and lacks the understory vegetation found in the surrounding woods. The path passes through another stone wall and soon reaches an intermittent stream. This crossing can be muddy. Just after crossing the stream, the path reaches a junction. The path going to the right goes to the Farmer's Cemetery on South Avenue (Route 30). You should take the path going to the left that returns up-stream in the hemlocks. Soon the path passes through a stone wall and you should keep bearing left avoiding the path on the right that goes east to Wellesley Street. Our path heads west and then bears right to a junction and an opening in a stone wall. Avoid the path to the left and pass through a gap in a stone wall onto a fire road that is situated between two stone walls. Turn left and follow along this fire road. If you turn to the right, the fire road soon becomes a path which goes to Wellesley Street near the Spellman Stamp Museum. At junction **9**, keep to your right following the fire road. Just beyond this junction, there are many tall hemlock trees. As you leave the hemlock woods, the canopy opens allowing more sun to reach the woodland floor. Note the change in the amount of understory vegetation. The fire road joins another fire road at junction **1**. This fire road is one of the former race tracks that General Paine used to train trotting horses at the end of the nineteenth century and to race motor cars during the first decade of this century. Junction **1**, **2**, **3**, and **4** are situated on this track which is a half-mile in length.

At junction **1**, turn to your right and continue along the former race track. Avoid the short trail to the right that leads to the parking lot at Alumnae Hall on the Regis College campus. Continue along the fire road avoiding a foot path and a wood road going to your right at junction **2**.

At junction **3**, note that the canopy trees are predominately beech and maple. Ferns are mainly interrupted and royal fern. Interrupted fern (*Osumunda claytoniana*) (Figure 5) is recognized by the fact that its fertile leaflets "interrupt" the sterile leaflets about the middle of the stem. Royal fern (*Osmunda regalis*) (Figure 6) looks like a fern from a distance, but close inspection of its leaflets show that they resemble those of a locust tree. Royal fern is a primitive

Fig 6

fern having had its origin in the late Paleozoic Era, 250 million years ago. The combination of swamp maple and these ferns indicates that this area is a wetland. Other plants near this junction are New York fern, low blueberry, and sassafras. New York fern has leaflets that taper to a point at both top and bottom. (New Yorkers burn their candles at both ends.) At junction **3**, turn off the former race track taking the fire road to the right which leads towards Chestnut Street. This fire road was used during the timber salvage operation after the 1938 hurricane. Salvaged wood was taken to a sawmill on the Sudbury River in Wayland.

This fire road starts up a valley. For a short distance, you may be able to see the intermittent stream on your left. As you rise into a drier area of forest, the trees in the canopy change to white birch, hickory, and beech. White, paper, or canoe Birch (*Betula papyrifera*) is readily recognized by its chalky-white bark that readily peels from the tree and can be separated into paper-thin layers. The northern Algonquins used its bark for canoes, cooking pots, dishes, trays, and a protective covering for their dwellings.

At junction J, a foot path crosses the fire road. This foot path runs from Regis College to Highland Street. Our journey continues along the fire road. We pass junction E where our north/south fire road crosses an east/west fire road. At junction E, we are in a dry woodland where the trees are mainly birch and black or red oak. Bracken fern and low blueberry form the main ground cover. White pines are also present. Beyond junction E, the fire road passes a trail on the left. Avoid this trail which leads to the water tank near the summit of Sanderson Hill. Continue along the fire road that drops down as it approaches Chestnut Street. Before reaching the gate at Chestnut Street, turn to your left along a well-trod woods path. The wood here is mainly maple and oaks. After leaving the fire road, it is about 150 feet to a gap in a stone wall. Pass through the wall. In another 120 feet, you arrive at the edge of a meadow. Follow the path for about 150 feet into the center of the meadow where you reach a crossing path. The path going to your right (north) enters into private land. Looking to the south, you can see an F & T arrow on a large white pine tree at the edge of the meadow. Head for this pine. As you cross the meadow, take time to notice the wildflower display. The path passes from the meadow, through a stone wall, and into the woods. The path gently ascends. Ignore the path on the left. After passing through a second stone wall, the path levels out on Sanderson Hill. Sanderson Hill does not have a distinct summit; but, it has a plateau for its summit. It was on this plateau that the Patriot's maintained a Revolutionary War beacon. A Town Water Department tank stands on this plateau. The small field by the water tank has interesting displays of our native wild flowers through the late spring, summer, and fall.

Just beyond the water tank, there is a fire hydrant along a fire road. At the hydrant turn left following the fire road as it rises slightly. Continue along the road through an area of mixed woodlands. Soon you will come to a junction where white birches can be seen ahead. This is junction **F**. I have maintained a breeding bird site here for several years. One can usually find a scarlet tanager family here in late May through June.

At junction **F**, turn to your right heading south to junction **G**. The fire road descends slightly and turns to the west at junction **G**. Continue following the fire road as it leads west. The fire road is more or less level for some distance. In this level area, there is a region where beech, grey birch, and black birch trees predominate. Black, cherry, or sweet birch (*Betula lenta*) grow up to 75 feet in height. The twigs are tasty to chew having a wintergreen taste and odor. The sap may be collected in the spring and used to prepare birch beer. The bark of this birch is blackish and breaks into flat, square plates with age.

Where the road starts to descend, there is a path leading to the left which you should follow.This path runs in an arc turning to the west and leading to a viewpoint, known as Sunset Corner, along Highland Street. Here, there is a plaque on a boulder that reads:

BICENTENNIAL   1976

THIS MEMORIAL WAS ERECTED BY THE TOWN OF WESTON AND THE WESTON FOREST AND TRAIL ASSOCIATION ON LAND DONATED TO THE TOWN IN 1955 BY THE CHARLES JACKSON PAINE FAMILY SO THAT THE VIEW TO THE WEST MIGHT BE ENJOYED BY FUTURE GENERATIONS

WEST BY SOUTH	REEVES HILL	2 MILES	406 ft
WEST	NOBSCOT HILL	8 MILES	602 ft
WEST BY NORTH	MT WACHUSETT	29 MILES	2106 ft
WEST NOR'WEST	MT MONADNOCK	52 MILES	3165 ft

Although Reeves Hill, Nobscot Hill, and Mt. Wachusetts may be seen on a clear day from this spot, Mt. Monadnock is hidden behind the pines on your right.

Continue across the view spot from this boulder. You will pass a path on your left leading to Highland Street and enter a pine wood. The path soon reaches the fire road, turn right and return to junction **G**. At junction G, the fire road turns to the left and heads to the north to Junction **F**. You should continue straight ahead along a foot path. In about 60 feet, you will pass through a gap in a stone wall. In another 30 feet, the foot path divides at a large white pine bearing an F & T sign. The second sign on this pine reads:

The Weston Boy Scout Troop 153 prepared these signs for an Eagle Scout Project managed by

David Kahler. The Troop placed these signs in
environmentally sensitive areas.

The trail on the right goes to junction **5** through
a wetland. Thus, we shall take the drier path to
the left to junction **J**. The canopy above this path
is initially oak and beech with an understory of
white pine, chestnut and sassafras. As the path
descends, white birch is found in the canopy
and bracken fern and low bush blueberry
among the ground cover. Soon, we reach a fire
road at junction **J** by a large hemlock. Turn to
your right following a fire road that ends at
junction **3**. Turn right on the fire road that is a
section of the former race track. At junction **4**,
turn to your right leaving the race track and
continue straight through junction **5** to junction
6. At junction **6**, leave the fire road to go straight
ahead along a foot path retracing your steps to
our starting place.

NOLTE TOWN FOREST
AND
VICINITY

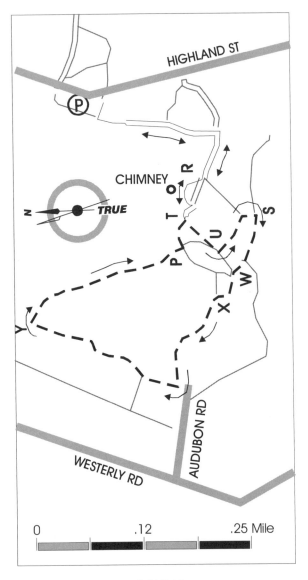

MAP 13

GENERAL INFORMATION:

Brenton H. Dickson, Jr. describes Highland Street about 1910 in his book, *Random Recollections*, as follows: "Going south on Highland Street there is better than a mile of uninhabited country, except for Nolte's camp, a long way off the road and used only in summer. This section, offered a variety of scenery and was ideal for anyone who wanted to take a walk in the quiet of the country."

Dorothea Nolte Kelley furnished the following information concerning the Nolte farm: "At the end of the nineteenth century, my father, George Nolte, bought a farm as a gift to his wife, Evelyn White. It was to be a summer home and the source of a little income. Since the only house on the property was needed for the farmer and his wife, a large rustic building was constructed at the south end of the property. It was completed about 1900, . . . We called it, 'The Bungalo'." In a second letter, Mrs. Kelley added that: "the large stone chimney is all that remains of the rustic building we called 'The Bungalo'. It was a dream house that we loved for many years . . . I spent every summer of my life there until it was demolished about 1917 or 18."

Mrs. Kelley's first letter continues: "Now that the forest has taken over, it is hard to believe what a pleasant place it was to me and my siblings.

"Besides numerous pastures and woods were: Three orchards, six hayfields, an ice pond, kitchen garden, corn field, a cool running brook, and a swamp. Near by was a cranberry bog (not a part of the property).

"This farm was approximately 70 acres, and ran south on Highland Street, and west on Elm Street (now Love Lane)."

The farmhouse mentioned by Mrs. Kelley, stands at 16 Love Lane. It was enlarged and used as a home by Mrs. Kelley's brother, Whitney R. Nolte, and his family until his death in 1974. In 1954, upon the death of their father, George Herbert Nolte, the farm was broken up. A section of woodland was designated as a memorial to Evelyn White Nolte, G. H. Nolte's first wife and mother of his children.

The Evelyn White Nolte Town Forest is a five acre plot just north of the Sunset Corner pull-off on the west side of Highland Street. Between Highland Street and Audubon Circle, there are 40 acres of Town Forest and two plots of land totaling five acres of Recreation Commission land which were a part of the Nolte farm. In addition, north of Audubon Circle, there is 8.50 acres of land designated as Town Conservation land. Thus, there is about 53 acres of Town land in this area.

PARKING:
At 1.0 mile south of Route 20 along Highland Street, there is convenient parking spot at the

pull-off by the large White Pine at Sunset Corner.

RECOMMENDED WALK:

This walk requires about an hour and a quarter. Some of the route is in wetlands and footwear should be appropriate to the season. Start from the Sunset Corner pulloff on Highland Street. Walk to the north end of the pulloff and take the path into the meadow. Turn to the south and walk parallel to Highland Street. The trees in the meadow are arbor vitae. These "trees of life" are members of the cypress family. They were one of the earliest trees to be exported from America to Europe after extracts cured the men of Jacques Cartier's Canadian expedition of a disease, probably scurvy. This tree is also known as northern white cedar although it is not a cedar. Cedars are old world trees. The Indians refer to this tree as canoe-wood as thin slabs of wood can be formed by pounding the ends of a short log until they separate along the annual rings. The wood is soft, flexible, and durable. Sticks can be used to start a fire by friction using the bark as the tinder.

Enter the woods bearing left and passing through an old stone wall. Soon, you pass an old borrow pit. The soil and gravel from the "borrow pit" were used in some construction project in the past. The birch tree in the mouth of the borrow pit is a yellow birch. The bark of this birch is shiny yellow or silvery gray with narrow horizontal lines along which small thin curls form as the bark peels. Examples of both bark colors occur here. Like black birch, the twigs give off a wintergreen odor. On the ground is lady fern (*Athyrium filix-femina*) (Figure 24) which is a common lacy-cut fern with many variations in the shape of the blade, the cutting of the leaflets, and color. The bottoms of the stems are usually slightly hairy.

Fig 24

From the borrow pit, the path follows an "S" curve uphill. When the path mets a fire road, go right along the road. In 100 feet, the path splits into three at junction **R**. Bear right, pass through a stone wall, and reach the chimney of "The Bungalo". As you leave the chimney bear right, pass through a stone wall, and return to the fire road. Turn to your right, pass through a gate in an old stone wall, and follow along the fire road to junction **T**. At this junction, bear to the left along a foot path which passes through a stone wall and leaves the fire road. The ground cover is principally Canada mayflower or wild lily-of-the-valley (*Maianthemum canadense*) (Figure 25).

Fig 25

In 150 feet, foot path reaches junction **U**. Turn to your left going slightly uphill to a stone wall. Pass through the stone wall and turn right at an unlabelled junction. Bear right. In about 40 feet, you will reach junction **S**. Again, go to your right. You are now in a pine plantation. Pass junction **W** and continue for 40 feet.to a gap in the stone wall on your left. Take the path leading to your left and pass through the stone wall. This path drops down into a fern filled valley, passes junction **X**, and then passes through a stone wall. Soon, you emerge onto Audubon Road just east of number 12. Go just past the mail box for number 12 and you will see a path leading down into the woods. Take this path and head north into a mixed woodland. Avoid the path leading to your left.

The path drops downhill, turns to the east, and crosses an intermittent stream. The path rises and descends again to cross another stream. Soon, the path enters upon a wetland and again crosses a stream. The path ends at junction **Y**. Turn to your right. The path passes through a wetland and crosses a shallow, wide stream. Soon, the path passes through a stone wall. Beyond this stone wall, there is a selection of clubmosses, ground pines, or running pines along the path. Fossils of these plants are known to date back to the Paleozoic Era, more than 300 million years ago. During the Carboniferous Period, the clubmosses and related genera existed in ferneries that were vast forest jungles. The spores from these fern allies were laid down in vast beds. These beds formed the geological seams from which man has mined coal, cannel coal, and jet. Jet is a compact coal which will take a high polish and is used for beads, buttons, decorative art and jewelry.

Modern clubmosses are small (6 to 12 inches in height), usually fully evergreen, perennial plants of upright, trailing, or creeping growth. Their many crowded, small leaves are all simple — never divided — stemless, and usually of uniform size. In most species, the leaves are arranged in rows, or ranks, of 4 to 14 around the erect or creeping stem in spirals, whorls, or opposite in overlapping or divergent growth forms. The leaves are narrow and pointed and some have a projecting bristly hair to each leaf. Their rootstocks increase in length each year and may be either above or below ground. Often, the growth of former years withers and dies or has been

Fig 26

collected for Christmas decorations and is sparse. But it may grow and spread faster than it dies; and, in this case, the colony may increase rapidly with time.

In this area, I found tree clubmoss (*Lycopodium obscurum*) (Figure 26) which looks like a tiny, shiny green, thickly branched pine tree. It is collected by model makers for use as pine trees and is collected for Christmas decoration. Also present is running pine or Christmas green (*L. complanatum*) whose common names give its appearance and one of its uses.

The angiosperms that are present as companions are indian cucumber root (*Medeola virginiana*) and starflower (*Trientalis borealis*) (Figure 27).

Fig 27

Surrounding this area of low plants is cinnamon fern (*Osmunda cinnamomea*) (Figure 4), royal fern (*O. regalis*) (Figure 6) as well as other ferns. The two osmundas are wetland indicator plants. This group of ferns originated in the final part of the Paleozoic Era, 250 million years ago. Their fossil remains are found on all seven continents, and, at present, they grow everywhere but in Antarctica.

The path slowly rises, crosses a wet spot where the path has been widened by trail bikers, passes through a stone wall, and then reaches junction **P**. Turn to the left and again pass through a stone wall. In 30 feet, you reach junction **T** at the end of the fire road leading to Highland Street. The first two paths on your left lead to the chimney. The third path on the left leads down to the borrow pit, up to the meadow, and to the pull-off on Highland Street.

Female Wild Turkey
(Meleagris gallopavo)

CHESTNUT STREET
AND
WOODLAND SCHOOL AREA

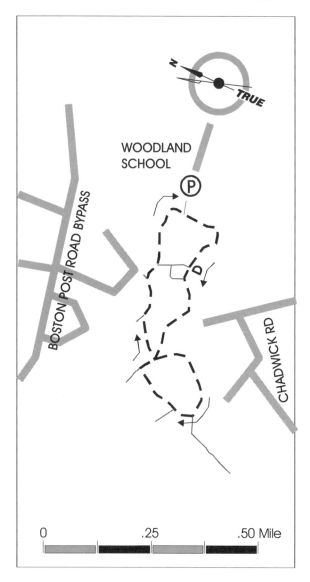

MAP 14

GENERAL INFORMATION:

As the glaciers melted away ten thousand years ago, Lake Sudbury formed between the hills to the south and an ice front to the north. The high level of the Weston stage of Glacial Lake Sudbury drained to the southeast through the valley south of Weston Reservoir where the Pine Brook Country Club links are situated. Most of the area described in this chapter is situated in this former lake bed. In historic time, this area was part of the drainage area of Three Mile Brook. This brook was harnessed for at least 200 years to furnish power to the mills just north of Crescent Street (Chapter 4). In the early 1930's, the present Boston Post Road By-pass was built through the valley of Three Mile Brook destroying its value as a source of power and leaving many swampy, poorly drained areas along the former valley of Three Mile Brook.

Country and Woodland Schools are built on land that was once a part of the Case Estate. To the west, the Town Conservation Land just to the east of Chandler Circle and Davenport Road was a part of the Paine Estate.

PARKING:

The most convenient parking area is the parking lot just west of the Woodland School. One may also park north of 78 Chestnut Street at the end of a fire road that leads into this area.

RECOMMENDED WALK:

Much of this area is a red maple swamp. During the spring and early summer, this area may be very wet and appropriate footwear should be worn. During fall and winter, it usually is drier. It requires about an hour to do this walk.

Park at the west end of the Woodland School Parking lot. At the southwest end of the lot, there is a woods road marked with F & T arrows. Head south along this road. On the left side of the road is a higher, dry area with a pine plantation with an understory of bracken. In May, Canada mayflower or wild lily-of-the-valley

Fig 28

(*Maianthemum   canadense*) (Figure   25),   starflower (*Trientalis borealis*) (Figure 27), and pink lady's slipper or moccasin flower (*Cypripedium acaule*) may be seen in bloom along the left side of the road. In early July, partridgeberry (*Mitchella repens*) (Figure 28) with its twinned flowers may be found in bloom. On the right side, the land slopes down into a swamp. A swamp is a wetland filled with growing shrubs and trees. Throughout New England, swamps appear much like an upland forest except that the shrubs and trees are growing in muck or standing water. Between the swamp and the road, the trees are mostly a mix of pin oaks and red maples. The road enters a mowed area at the edge of the Arnold Arboretum.

At this mowed area, turn right along the edge of the mowed area. Follow along the mowed area for about 130 feet. By a pin oak, you will come to a cleared road through an area of buckthorn (*Rhamus* sp.). Turn right decending along a trail into a red maple swamp where you cross over a pair of old concrete bridges. Between these bridges, one may find sphagnum moss. Sphagnum or peat moss is used for packing nursery stock as it holds moisture and keeps roots fresh. Chopped sphagnum is an excellent cover for a seedbed or an addition to soil to maintain moisture and porosity. Formerly, this moss was wrapped in cheesecloth, sterilized, and used as a packing for seeping wounds. Throughout this walk, you will see sphagnum in the moister areas.

By the second bridge, you may find lady fern (*Athyrium filix-femina*) (Figure 24). In late summer, just beyond the second bridge, the strong fragrance emanates from sweet pepperbush (*Clethra alinifolia*) (Figure 12) with its long racemes of white flowers. The trail rises onto a high drier area and comes to junction **D**. Normally, avoid the trail to the right which goes to Linwood Cemetery; however, you may wish to go this way if the water level is very high. At junction **D**, continue straight ahead for about 100 feet. Note the fern bed to your left, it contains Massachusetts fern (*Thelypteris* *simulata*). It is a rare fern and was first described in 1894. Here the trail splits, take the branch to the left which passes through a wetland. This section of trail is almost always wet and is an excellent site to observe the wetland ferns - cinnamon, interrupted, marsh, royal, and sensitive fern may all be found along this section of trail. There are also skunk cabbage and many jack-in-the-pulpits. There are two wooden bridges in this area. After crossing this wetland you reach a drier area with many examples of Solomon's seals (*Polygonatum* sp.) (Figure 2) and false Solomon's seal or wild spikenard (*Smilacina racemosa*) (Figure 3).

Fig 29

You will reach a stand of 100 foot white pines. Here four trails come together. Keep to the extreme left to follow a trail around a vernal pool and to return to this spot. The trail soon comes to the outlet from the vernal pool. The shrub in the pool is buttonbush (*Cephalanthus occidentalis*) (Figure 29). The round, ball-like structures are flower heads formed from small white, tubular flowers about 0.3 inch long with a long, protruding style which give the flower clusters a fuzzy appearance. Buttonbush flowers in August. Seeds form in the autumn.

From the outlet of the vernal pool, the trail rises from the wetland on to a higher area of glacial till. Glacial till is a non-stratified sediment of varying grain size (clay to boulders) deposited by the glaciers. This deposit extends south over most of the Highland Street Town Forest.

The trail soon enters drier woodland and parallels a stone wall before passing through a wall near a wall corner and heading west. The trail ends on a woods road coming from Chestnut Street to our south. At the junction, notice the oak tree. The leaves typically have 4 to 6 pairs of large rounded teeth, are wedged shaped at their base, and are usually white and hairy on the underside. This oak is known as the swamp white oak. It is the only oak in which the stems on the acorns are longer than the leaf stems.

Turn north (right) at this junction. On the left, is Chandler Circle. The trail descends and soon crosses an inlet of the vernal pool. The open area to your right is the vernal pool. The trail continues through a hickory, maple and oak wood. It passes through a stone wall. Just after entering a stand of tall white pines, the trail reaches a junction. You can see that the trail to the left leads west to Davenport Road. Turn to the right (east). In about 125 feet, you again come to the junction where the four trails met.

At this junction take the trail to the extreme left and head north. Once again you will soon find yourself in a red maple swamp. On leaving this swamp, you are on the southerly edge of

Linwood Cemetery. Turn to the right and follow
along the road for about 225 feet. Just past a
large red maple, you should now see a F & T
arrow. Keep to the southerly edge of the mowed
area. On a large white pine to your right, you
should now see a F & T arrow. Reenter the
swamp. You will reach a junction in about 100
feet after leaving the cemetery. Turn to your left.
(If you go right you will reach junction **D**.) Pass
though a wall near a wall corner. Cross over two
old concrete bridges. After the second bridge,
you   pass   through   Japanese   knotweed
(*Polygonum cuspidatum*), an invasive alien plant
which is difficult to control. Note the large pin
oak along the right of the trail. It is about 10 feet
in circumference. The parking lot from which
we started can be seen ahead.

FISKE TOWN FOREST

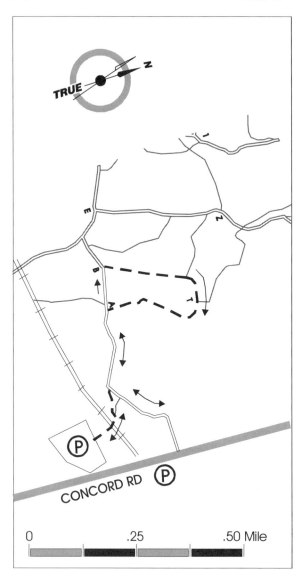

MAP 15

GENERAL INFORMATION:
The Fiske Town Forest lies in the southeastern corner of the Jericho Town Forest. It was obtained from the heirs of Gertrude H. Fiske in 1962. It protects a portion of the recharge area of the Cambridge Stony Brook Reservoir.

PARKING:
One may start this walk from either Concord Road or from Jericho Village. To park:

1) Along Concord Road. Drive down the Dead End at the north end of the bridge over the abandoned railroad and park. Follow the sidewalk to 25 feet north of the Laxfield Road entrance and cross Concord Road to utility pole # 24. Pass around an iron gate and enter a fire road. This fire road goes to the west through a pine plantation.

2) In Jericho Village. Drive west on Jericho Road parking just beyond the garage numbered 40. There is a path by the large oak situated between the two garages. This path leads to a path under the Boston Edison High Tension Line. Turn to your right (east) on a trail that passes a high tension tower and continue east. Just before the next high tension tower, there is a path on the left which leads north into the woods. Almost immediately, you come to a junction. Bear left. The path soon passes through a

stone wall and joins the fire road
mentioned above which originates on
Concord Road. Go left. Directions for
this walk continue in the fourth
paragraph below.

RECOMMENDED WALK:
The time of this walk is about an hour and a
quarter.

From the west side of Concord Road, enter a fire
road by utility pole # 24 passing around an iron
gate. This fire road starts on private land;
however, residents have a right to enter the
Fiske Town Forest along this route.

Follow the fire road as it descends into an area
of alternating dry area and wetlands. Two foot
paths join the road from the south (left). These
paths come from Jericho Village.

In the region of the foot paths, red maple and
red oaks become more common. The forest floor
is covered by low   blueberry and many
wildflowers. In Spring, Canada mayflower or
wild lily-of-the-valley (*Maianthemum canadense*)
(Figure 25) and starflower (*Trientalis borealis*)
(Figure 6) bloom here. In early July,
partridgeberry (*Mitchella repens*) (Figure 28)
blooms. From June through the first heavy frost,
knotweeds or smartweeds (*Polygonum*) are in
bloom; and, from mid-August to frost, sharp-
leaved, mountain, or whorled Aster (*Aster
acuminatus*) is in bloom. The most common fern

in this area is evergreen, leatherleaf or marginal woodfern (*Dryopteris marginalis*) (Figure 20) which remains green all year although it may burn out in the heat of summer or dry out in the cold of winter. The tall mid story shrub with black berries is a buckthorn (*Rhamnus* sp.).

Soon the fire road is flanked on both sides by stone walls. The road crosses Cherry Brook and enters the Fiske Town Forest. Ninety feet after crossing the brook, there is a path which we will use on our return. Continue on the fire road for 30 more feet to reach junction **A**. At the junction bear right and continue some 350 feet to junction **B**. At this second junction, take the woods path to your right leaving the fire road. The shrubs growing under the bracken are low bush blueberry. Few berries are found on these bushes because either insufficient light reaches the floor of the forest or they are eaten as soon as they ripen.

The path rises and passes through a stone wall. To the right, in a patch of Canada mayflower or wild lily-of-the-valley, there is also a clubmoss, running pine or Christmas green (*Lycopodium complanatum*) (Figure 22). In this area, there is also a boulder covered with sphagnum moss. The sphagnum completely covers the boulder and is usually sopping wet illustrating one property of sphagnum moss; that is, it can hold eight times its volume of water even when it is above the surroundings.

Further on, the path starts to drop down a small
slope. On the left-hand side of the path, there is
pipsissewa   or   prince's   pine   (*Chimaphila
umbellata*) (Figure 18) which is a member of the
wintergreen family. It flowers at the beginning
of summer and its flowers resemble umbrellas.
On the right side, there is a clubmoss, tree
clubmoss (*Lycopodium   obscurum*) (Figure 26),
which resembles a six inch high, thickly
branched pine tree topped by oversized erect
cones.

You will reach a "Y" in the path. Bear to your
right, avoiding the path going left which passes
through a stone wall. Continuing along the path
you soon come to junction **T**. Again, avoid the
path to your left and go to your right
passing through a stone wall. Just
beyond the wall, there is an area with
lots of haircap moss. The path again
rises as it heads to the south and
passes many clumps of haircap moss
(Figure 30). Haircap moss is a
bryophyte and is a nonvascular plant.
It lacks true foliage, true roots, a
highly developed internal circulation
system, and a cuticle, the waxy outer
layer that helps higher plants resist
                                                     Fig 30
water loss. On the floor of this moist forest,
water loss is not a problem. Look carefully at the
haircap moss to see the thin capsule-bearing
stalks that resemble a head covered by an old-
fashioned sunbonnet. These stalks rise from a
lower section that resembles a tiny juniper tree.

Strange as it may seem, you are seeing two different stages of the plant living at the same time. The upper portion (the stalk and capsule) is the spore-producing generation. When the spores are released and fall upon moist ground, they give rise to a lower portion which develops gametes (sex cells) which fuse in the soil to produce a new spore-producing generation (the stalk and capsule).

In the Phylum Bryophyta (mosses and liverworts), the gamete-forming generation forms the plant which attracts our notice and unless we look carefully, we readily miss the spore forming generation. However, in the flowering or vascular plants, the spore forming generation forms the eye-catching flowers that gardeners cherish; while the gamete-forming generation does its thing hidden within the pistil of the flower.

Many people see ferns all their life without realizing that these plants are only the spore-forming generation and only half of the full life cycle. The gamete-forming generation consists of a microscopic structure called the prothallus which is impossible to see amongst the leaf litter of the forest floor. (Many ferns also reproduce asexually by underground rhizomes. This route results in clones of the mother plant and avoids all that stuff about generations and sex.)

The path drops down again and passes through a stone wall. In this area, one can find the two clubmosses, running pine or Christmas green and tree clubmoss. Here, among the ferns are found cinnamon, Massachusetts, and New York fern. Cinnamon fern (*Osmunda cinnamomea*) (Figure 4) is one of the most common ferns in our area found mainly in moist, shady places. It is usually three or more feet high, coarse in appearance, and grows in arching circular clusters. Marsh fern (*Thelypteris palustris*) (Figure 31) is a common fern about eighteen inches in height and about six inches wide. New York Fern (*Thelypteris noveboracensis*) (Figure 32) is more delicate than marsh fern and its leaves are tapered at both ends. (Remember: New Yorkers burn their candles at both ends.)

Fig 31

The path soon reaches the fire road. Turn to your left and head back toward Concord Road. If you are going to Concord Road, remember to bear left, avoiding the trails to the right. On the other hand, to return to Jericho Village, bear right on either of the two paths, cross the rail bed, and then turn right going to the high tension tower and the path into Jericho Village.

Fig 32

16

JERICHO TOWN FOREST

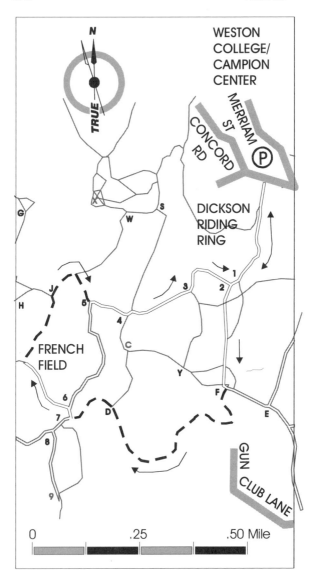

MAP 16

GENERAL INFORMATION:

Jericho Town Forest protects a portion of the recharge area of the Cambridge Stony Brook Reservoir. Much of this area is drained by Cherry Brook. This brook meanders south along Warren Avenue before turning north to College Pond before eventually joining Stony Brook. There are several areas of bedrock outcrops; but, the greater part of the area either consists of deposits from the glacial Lake Sudbury or is swamp of recent origin.

There are many places in eastern Massachusetts named Jericho. Most of these places were named in the seventeenth and eighteenth century when reading was learned from the Holy Bible. Thus, the selection of names was often based on Biblical sources. To one living at that time, Jericho meant either "a place of retirement or concealment" or "a place far distant and out of the way". In his *History of the Town of Weston, Massachusetts*, Colonel Lamson reprints the tale of one British spy who supposedly took refuge in Jericho swamp just before the Battle of Lexington and Concord. The Biblical story related in II Samuel, 10:1 - 5, tells the story of King David's emissaries who were taken to be spies. As punishment, the emissaries' had one-half of their beards shaved off and one-half of the garments cut off in the middle, "even to their buttocks" before being sent home. King David advised them "to tarry in Jericho" until their beards had regrown.

In the first half of the twentieth century, the area was one of estates and farms. Other than stone walls, little evidence of man's activity remains in the area. Until about 1970, one could readily detect the cranberry bogs in this area.   John Cronin, whose father managed the Weston College Farm and who has lived next to the former Weston College potato field for most of his life, told me that to earn pocket money during the 1930's, he picked and sold cranberries from the local bogs.

PARKING:
Starting from the junction of Concord Road and Merriam Street, drive 0.4 mile along Concord Road and turn into the road going to the right to the College Pond Parking lot. Once on this road, bear to the right and you will reach the parking lot at College Pond. This is the starting place for this walk.

Other access points to the Jericho Town Forest are available. In Wayland, one may park at the end of either Old Weston Road or Wildwood Road. In Weston, one can park on Warren Avenue near Gun Club Lane (a private way) or use various pullouts along Concord Road.

RECOMMENDED WALK:
About one to two hours are required to complete this walk.

Starting from the College Pond Parking lot, walk back toward Concord Road. At the junction of the entrance road with the asphalt road leading into the Campion Center land, continue straight ahead on a path. The path reaches the stone wall along Concord Road and follows it to an opening opposite 288 Concord Road. Cross Concord Road and walk northwest along the roadside for 130 feet until you reach the Ruth B. Dickson Memorial Ring gate.

Pass through the gate and enter the Ring area keeping to the left along the fire road. When the fire road reaches the woodland, bear left on the fire road and continue into the woods. Continue along this fire road which once led to former the Pine Hill Poultry Farm. The road enters a pine plantation. In the late 1960's, goshawks nested in this area. This area was closed during the nesting season as the goshawks protected their nest and nestlings by flying straight into your face with their talons projecting. Those who experienced these flights agreed that these magnificent raptors had a very effective way of discouraging human intrusion into their nursery.

At junction **1**, there is a path on the left side of the fire road. Take this path. The ground cover along the path is Canada mayflower or wild lily-of-the-valley (*Maianthemum canadense*) (Figure 25) which blooms during May. Deeper into the pine plantation, there is little ground cover due to the lack of light. Soon our path is crossed by an east/west path. Ignore the crossing path and continue straight ahead. The path drops down and passes through a stone wall entering a mixed woodland of red maple and white pine. The path then terminates on a fire road.

Go left along this central fire road until you reach junction **F**. At junction **F**, avoid the fire road which bears to the left and a path which leads to the right, go straight ahead along what appears to be a fire road but soon becomes a path. I believe that the poultry farm was in the area west of the stone wall which parallels our path on the left. In Spring, Canada mayflower or wild lily-of-the-valley and starflower (*Trientalis borealis*) (Figure 27) bloom along the path. The path passes through a stone wall and enters land formerly a part of Mrs. Marion Farnsworth Boynton's Exmoor Farm.

Mrs. Boynton bought the Harrington Farm in 1920 and left it in 1954 upon her marriage. After World War I, she visited England and spent considerable time riding and tramping in Exmoor. Exmoor lies in Devon and Somerset Counties in England just south of the Bristol Channel. Exmoor was a Royal Hunting Forest until the time of Victoria. John Knight, who had made his fortune in iron, purchased the forest and converted it into open, productive farmland. Exmoor became a National Park in 1954.

In remembrance of her English sojourn, Mrs. Boynton named her Weston estate Exmoor Farm. She lived a gracious, self-sufficient life in

Weston. During World War II, she enlarged the Harrington house and sheltered children who had been evacuated from England. Life at Exmoor is documented in the files of the Historical Society and in the Oral Histories of Philip D. Bassett and Jenny Kroll available at the Weston Library.

The path parallels the stone wall for 70 feet before leaving Exmoor. The path bears right and passes beyond the stone wall. At the wall corner, there is New York fern (*Thelypteris noveboracensis*) (Figure 32). This delicate yellow-green fern is tapered at both ends. Remember the mnemonic that New Yorkers burn their candle at both ends. Twenty feet beyond the wall, lady fern (*Athyrium filix-femina*) (Figure 24) borders the path. This is a large, lacy-cut, and showy fern with a slight hairiness at the bottom of the stems. In about 50 feet, the path passes a moister area with cinnamon fern (*Osmunda cinnamomea*) (Figure 6). Where the path rises slightly to a drier area, one can find evergreen, leatherleaf, or marginal woodfern (*Dryopteris marginalis*) (Figure 20) growing. The path then drops slightly to a moister place and one finds both cinnamon fern (*Osmunda cinnamomea*) (Figure 4) and royal fern (*Osmunda regalis*) (Figure 6). The osumunda family originated at the end of the Paleozoic area, 250 million years ago. Despite their time of origin, these sporophytes seem to be more prevalent and successful than at any other time in their long history. We may hope that our species can achieve such success. In spring, one can find blooming jack-in-the-pulpits (*Arisaema triphyllum*) (Figure 33) in this wetland; and, in fall, one can find dense clusters of scarlet red berries, which is their fruit. The canopy above us is now mainly red maple, signaling, as do the osmunda that we are in wetland. The path splits where it crosses Cherry Brook, an intermittent stream in this area, and rejoins on the far side of the stream. The path now rises from the swamp

and the canopy changes from red maple to red and scarlet oak signaling drier woods. The ground cover is mainly shrubs from the heath family, including low blueberry. As we proceed, white pines again are found in the canopy. At junction **D**, avoid the path going to the right and into the wet land, continuing straight ahead on the drier path. The path soon ends on a

Fig 33

fire road. Turn right and continue for 150 feet along the fire road, which passes by a wetland before reaching junction **6**.

At junction **6**, turn left along a fire road which rises over a ridge before descending into a wetland. On either side of the fire road just before crossing the wetland there is a station of interrupted fern (*Osmunda claytoniana*) (Figure 5). The fire road crosses an intermittent stream.

Before fill was placed here for the road, there was a low stone dam. The dam stored water to keep the area to the left moist all summer for the growing of cranberries. In the 1960's, one could harvest a few berries here.

The fire road now rises into French Field. The Town Forest Committee decided many years ago to keep this area mowed to provide an open field. Turn right and walk to the north end of the field. At the north end of the field, you pass through a stone wall and reenter the forest. By the wall, there are bracken fern and shrubs of the heath family that indicate a drier spot in the forest. The canopy here is a mixture of red maple, red oak, and white pine. The path continues to junction J.

At junction J, bear to your right. In about 100 feet, the trail passes through a wetland with its cinnamon fern. Further on, the path separates at an intermittent stream crossing. The pedestrian route is to the left where there are stepping stones, while the equestrian route is to the right where wading is necessary. Thirty feet beyond the stream, the pedestrian trail crosses the equestrian route and continues straight ahead. In another 100 feet you pass through a stone wall and go another 70 feet before passing through a second stone wall. The path goes along with the stone wall on your left before reaching junction **5**, at a fire road. At this junction, there is a stand of cinnamon and interrupted fern.

Turn to your left at junction **5**, and go along the
fire road. The fire road soon enters a pine
plantation. The forester who first advised the
Town Forest Committee recommended planting
of white pine plantations. The Committee soon
decided that the lack of understory growth
under the pines made a dull walk. A new
forestry program was devised which
emphasized the encouragement and harvest of
hardwoods. This program continues at present. I
believe that the fire road passes through the
former poultry farm between junctions **5** and **4**.

At junction **4**, keep along the fire road that soon
crosses a wetland under a canopy of red maple.
In winter and early spring, this wetland appears
as if a bulldozer had been driven down stream.
This is a spillway which once connected two
sections of glacial Lake Sudbury. Today, it is
part of the course of Cherry Brook. Beyond the
wetland, there is a small borrow pit on the right
just before you reach junction **3**.

At junction **3**, bear left on the fire road until you
reach junction **2** where this fire road ends on
another fire road. Turn to the left on the fire
road. This fire road soon passes junction **1** and
goes to the Dickson Memorial Ring. Walk out to
Concord Road, cross to the far side where you
may find a narrow path, and turn right
following either the path or the edge of the road.
Opposite the mailbox for 288 Concord Road,
there is an opening in the stone wall on your

left. Enter and follow the path back to the College Pond Parking Lot.

Trunk of the cut-leafed beech
(*Fagus sylvatica laciniata*)
Case Municipal Purposes Land

WALK

17

COLLEGE
CONSERVATION AREA

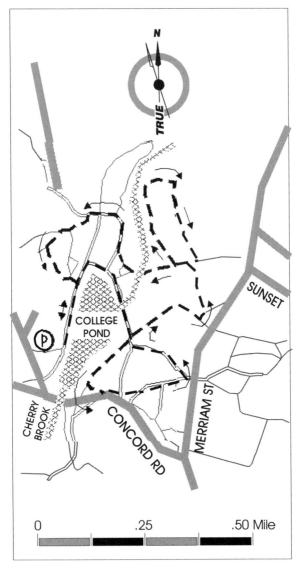

MAP 17

GENERAL INFORMATION:

In 1977, the Town bought 146 acres of land from Weston College. Until this transaction, all conservation lands were bought with funds furnished from Weston residents. In this single case, some funds were obtained from Massachusetts Self-Help Program. This land, commonly referred to as the Weston College Land, lies to the east of the present Campion Residence and Renewal Center. At the western boundary, the Town has constructed two soccer fields. The northern boundary lies along the line of Cherry Brook, the eastern is Merriam Street, and the southern is Concord Road.

In 1921, this area was occupied by two estates that were purchased by the Society of Jesus. Then the Jesuits built Weston College, a seminary for the training of priests. From 1924 until 1978, as many as 200 seminarians were involved in the seven year program. In 1978, the seminary program moved to the Harvard School of Theology and became the Weston School of Theology. The former Weston College became the Campion Center with a Jesuit Infirmary for retired priests and a Retreat House for interested persons. The Chapel at the Campion Center is known for its excellent acoustics and is used for recording both orchestral and vocal music. If you wish to view the Chapel, contact the receptionist at the Campion Center before your visit.

North of the Campion Center is the Weston Observatory, Department of Geology and Geophysics, Boston College. Michael Ahern, S.J, founded the Observatory in 1930. Its research programs have continued under the able direction of Daniel J. Linehan, S.J., then of James W. Skehan, S.J., and, at present, of Dr. John Ebel. The Observatory operates the 29-station New England Seismic Network to monitor regional earthquake activity. The Observatory records, locates, and computes the magnitudes of some 50+ regional earthquakes annually. At the Observatory, the seismographs are a part of the Worldwide Standard Seismographic Network. These seismographs record over 100 significant earthquakes over the world each year. The Observatory participated in the Joint Verification Experiment to develop methods to distinguish between nuclear explosions, small explosions, and earthquakes. This research was important to assure that verification of nuclear explosions was possible and lead to the 1988 Nuclear Test Ban Treaty. The staff has been actively involved in regional geological and plate tectonic studies of our region. There is an interesting display of rocks in front of the Observatory. If you contact the Observatory and a staff member is free, a tour of the Museum can be arranged which includes a viewing of the seismographic array.

The brick house at 319 Concord Road, now a part of the Campion Center, was built in 1906 for Grant Walker, a Boston businessman and investor, after the original wood house on the site burned down. The estate included 131 acres. A year after Mr. Walker's death, his widow sold the estate to the Society of Jesus and moved to Lincoln.

Merriam Street is named after Herbert Merriam. Herbert was a son of Charles Merriam who came to Weston in 1824 and operated a store across from the First Parish Church. Charles was a selectman in 1835, gave gifts to the library in 1859 and 1865 and, in 1865, established the "Merriam Fund for the Benefit of the Silent Poor of Weston." Herbert Merriam, a Boston businessman, built his estate at the corner of Concord Road and Merriam Street. His land extended on both sides of the two roads and to College Pond and was about 230 acres. Along the road to the former brush dump was a dairy barn that is said to have been "one of the largest in Middlesex Country." This barn was built in 1876 and burnt down on October 30, 1926. No animals were lost in the fire. Pictures of the barn can be found in *The Weston Historical Society Bulletin*, Vol. XVII, No 1 (October 1980) and No. 2 (January 1981). A dairy herd was housed in the big barn. Horse barn and several chicken houses were situated just east of Merriam Street on the Municipal Purposes Land.

PARKING:
There are two parking areas along Concord Road. Starting from the junction of Concord Road and Merriam Street:

1) Drive 0.3 mile along Concord Road, on the right, there is a pull off by the Town's orchard.

2) Drive 0.4 mile along Concord Road and turn into the road going to the right. Once on this road, bear to the right and you will reach the parking lot at College Pond. This is the starting place for this walk.

white violet 2:20   4:10

RECOMMENDED WALK:

This walk requires about two hours to walk around most of College Pond, to visit the orchard and the Merriam Barn site, to follow Cherry Brook north before returning to walk over a bedrock outcrop.

After parking in the College Pond parking lot, walk over to the tennis courts. Inset into a boulder in front of the courts is a plaque, which reads:

> Harold G. "Red"
> Travis Courts
> Dedicated
> Sept. 25, 1984

For many years, Red Travis edited The Weston Historical Society Bulletin.

Pass through the gate to the right of the tennis courts and walk along the road. Just beyond the tennis courts, on the left, there is a second commemorative boulder, which reads:

> Gustic Park
> In Memory of
> Mr. Frank Gustic, Sr.
> Dedicated May 5, 1984

Mr. Gustic was Commissioner of the Men's Softball League. He and his sons served in this capacity for about 30 years.

On the hill to your left is the main building of the Campion Center. Closer to us are a baseball field and several soccer fields.

The road soon enters woodland and comes to a road junction. At the junction, bear to the right. The road is now part of an embankment that separates College Pond on the right from the wetland to the left. On reaching the spillway, look over the pond. In spring and fall, ducks are often found feeding on the pond. In summer, the pond is overgrown with water chestnut, a very invasive alien. In August, the common shrub growing along the shore is buttonbush (*Cephalanthus occidentalis*) (Figure 29). The round, ball-like structures are flower heads formed from small white, tubular flowers about 0.3 inch long with a long, protruding style which give the flower clusters a fuzzy appearance. Its spherical seedheads form in late summer. Also, in late summer, there are sweet-scented water lily (*Nymphaea odorata*) (Figure 34) growing in the pond and pickerelweed (*Pontederia cordata*) (Figure 35) with a spike of small purple flowers above its heart-shaped leaves growing near to the shore.

Fig 34

Continue along the road for about 80 feet before turning to the right and following a path along the shore of the pond. These woods are largely of mixed pines. Look carefully near the base of the trunks of the pine trees and along the ground where their roots might be found. You should see some clusters of stems rising about a foot above the ground with flowers at their tips. Most of the year, these stems and flowers are black; but, in moister times from July to October, they may appear to be tawny yellow to red in color. These plants are pinesap or false beechdrops (*Monotropa hypopithys*) (Figure 36) and are related to Indian pipe. These plants are members of the wintergreen family, which during their evolution lost the ability to produce chlorophyll, the green pigment of plants. Authorities disagree whether these plants are parasites or

Fig 35

saprophytes. However, there is little doubt that they tap the roots of other plants and steal the nutrients that are needed for their survival. Having no need to produce their own food via photosynthesis they have lost chlorophyll and their leaves have atrophied to tiny bracts which can be seen along the stem. Before fertilization, their flowers hang their heads down. Once fertilized, the flowers point upwards. Their seed is scattered when an animal brushes the plants knocking out the seed.

On the drier hillside to the left, the ground cover is mostly Canada mayflower or wild lily-of-the-valley (*Maianthemum canadense*) (Figure 25).

Along the shore of the pond are patches of marsh fern (*Thelypteris palustris*).

The path rises and bears left as it enters into a stand of oaks. Near the high point, go left on a path leading away from the pond and going into an orchard. Land's Sake maintains this orchard for the Conservation Commission. The path continues along Concord Road with the orchard on the left.

Fig 36

At an iron pipe gate to Concord Road, turn left and follow along a buckthorn hedge. Turn right into the pinewood when you see a pine bearing an F & T arrow. This path soon ends on an old farm road. Turn left and follow the farm road.

Just as an open meadow appears on the right,
you will notice, on the left, the stonework wall
of the stock pens that were just south of the
Merriam barn. When you reach the iron pipe
gate on the road leading into the former brush
dump and compost area, turn left along the
dump road which also follows the route of an
old farm road. In about 100 feet, you will be at
the foot of the stone ramp supported by
buttresses that led to the third story of the barn.
This ramp was used by hay wagons to bring hay
to the loft. Parallel and adjacent to this ramp is a
second ramp without buttresses that led to the
second story. Behind it you can see more stone
work remains of the ground floor.

Continue straight along the road. When you
reach the attendant's shelter, continue down the
left side of the grassy slope toward College
Pond. At the bottom of the slope, head back to
the right toward the dam watching to the right
for an F & T arrow. It is about 75 feet beyond the
foot of the slope on a pine tree and a short
distance before the spillway. Turn in on this
path which follows Cherry Brook as it flows to
the north. Loop 40mw.

This path is bordered on the left by cinnamon
fern (*Osmunda cinnamomea*) (Figure 4) in the
wetland and by evergreen, leatherleaf, or
marginal woodfern (*Dryopteris marginalis*)
(Figure 20) on the drier and higher slope. It is
useful to recognize cinnamon fern as its

preferred habitat is damp and waterlogged locations. Avoid walking where this fern grows to keep your feet dry. The path passes through a stone wall into a wet spot and through another stone wall onto a drier area before coming to a road. Note the changes in vegetation as you move between dry and wet areas.

Bear to your left onto the road avoiding the road leading to the right and Merriam Street. Also, on your right, there is a pond. If you pass quietly, you may find either a great blue heron or green-backed heron feeding on frogs from this pond. In late April, this pond is a good site for finding pollywogs.

The road passes over the outlet from the pond and then comes to a junction. The path to the right goes to Merriam Street; take the path to the left. The path soon broadens and is bordered on the left by a line of very large white pines. The white birches at some distance beyond these pines are on the bank of Cherry Brook. Just beyond these pines, the path passes through a stone wall. There is old dump along this wall — beware of broken glass. The path continues for about 300 feet before ending on a road. Turn to the left and walk about 30 feet along the road before turning to your right on a path leading into the pines. This path soon reaches a hemlock grove along an intermittent watercourse. Note that you pass through some cinnamon ferns just as you reach the hemlocks. As noted above, the change in vegetation warns you that this is a moister area with richer soil. The hemlocks form a dense canopy above you. One result of this dense canopy is that a hemlock grove is noticeably cooler than the surrounding woods and lacks the understory vegetation found in the surrounding woods.

The path rises out of the hemlock grove into pinewoods. Note how much more light reaches the forest floor. A result of the additional light is that the principal understory plants in this region are young white pine trees. If you look at the white pines, you will note that there is a ring of several branches around the trunk, the usual number is five, then there is a space, then another ring, and so on almost to the top of the tree. Each ring of branches marks the end of a year's growth. Thus, one can tell the age of a white pine by counting the number of rings of branches. When white pines grow under ideal conditions, the space between the rings of branches is about 18 inches. Thus, if you count the rings of branches and make an estimate for the lower part of the trunk where the branches have been lost, your count times 18 inches gives you a good estimate of the height of the white pine. The number of rings of branches plus the estimate for the lower part of the trunk equals the age of the white pine. Many of the smaller white pines along the path do not show 18" of growth between branch rings showing the effect of competition with the larger pines for light and minerals.

Our path loops back to the right to the road through the pine plantation. Keep bearing right at junctions. There are two paths leaving to the left which you should avoid. Note the bracken fern along the path that indicates that this plantation is a dry woodland. You will reach a junction. Take the right-hand branch and you will reach the road in about 50 feet. Continue along the road passing the entrance to the paths just traveled and crossing Cherry Brook on a bridge. Beyond the bridge, keep right at the next two junctions. You will be passing through the site of a former piggery. Before 1965, Weston was the site of many piggeries. As these pigs were fed garbage from Waltham and Weston, the piggeries gave the town a distinctive bouquet in summer. *Bellwort, bloodwort, Wild geranium   Trillium*

Soon the path reaches a fire road. Keep to your right, walking along the road, and avoiding a right turn just before reaching a field. Upon reaching the field, follow the path going straight ahead, cross a road which goes to the Campion Center sewerage beds, and head for a red oak at the end of a white pine hedge row. Pass by the oak heading for the vegetated edge where the path enters a wood. After entering the woods, go about 60 feet and take the first left. The path rises to the top of a bedrock outcrop. Avoid the path descending into an open field on your right by keeping to your left. This trail meanders to the edge of a soccer field. Keeping in the woods, turn left and walk about 70 feet before going right on a path. This path meets the road from the tennis courts. Turn to your right and return to our starting place.

WALK

18

OGILVIE
TOWN FOREST

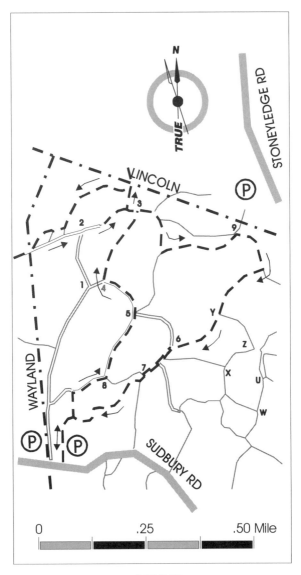

MAP 18

GENERAL INFORMATION:
The Ogilvie Town Forest started with the acquisition of 48 acres from the family of Beriah L. Ogilvie in 1960. Since that time an additional 10 acquisitions have brought the total area of this forest to 196 acres. The area includes vernal ponds and wetlands separated by bedrock ridges. This area tells us an interesting story.

In the lead article of the 76th Annual New England Intercollegiate Geologic Conference published in 1984, Patrick J. Barosh states, "Southeastern New England contains some of the most interesting, varied, and complex geology of all of North America." Since 1970, much of the geologic story of this region has been reinvestigated providing many interesting luncheon discussions with my colleagues who practice geology. I will attempt to relate from a layman's standpoint a simplification of these discussions.

In the late Precambrian, there was a collision between the Paleo-North American and Paleo-African plates forming a single super continent. This "collision zone" is situated in Essex, Middlesex, and Worcester counties and is the largest fault zone in the United States. The northern boundary of this fault zone runs roughly from Newburyport along Interstate 495 and then west on Route 2. The western boundary lies along the line of Interstates 190, 290, and 395 to Long Island Sound. The southern boundary of the fault zone runs very roughly

from Rowley to Interstate 95 and then out the
Massachusetts Turnpike (Interstate 90) to
Webster.

One major fault system in this zone is named
after Bloody Bluff in Lexington where a major
skirmish occurred on April 19, 1775. The Bloody
Bluff fault zone runs from Newburyport down
to Webster where it connects to other fault
systems. This fault system was active from the
late Precambrian Era into the Mesozoic Era at a
time when continental plates coalesced to form a
super continent. The fault forms the
southeastern boundary of the "collision zone".
Roughly 200 million years ago, the super
continent broke up with the opening up of the
North Atlantic basin just east of the old
"collision zone". This left a relic terrain attached
to southeastern New England that was once
attached to North Africa. This terrain was
further modified by the Pleistocene glaciation of
3 million to 10 thousand years ago. Repeated
bulldozing of the surface by glaciation stripped
most the softer material off the bedrock.
Haphazard redeposition of the well-mixed
softer materials left a great variety of unsorted
material on the surface. Since the melting of the
ice, many hollows left in the topography have
filled with soft sediments and peat.

The Bloody Bluff fault system is about a mile in
width. Along Route 117, as one enters Lincoln,
one can see wetland covering areas of shattered
bedrock. The wetland is bordered on the west

by a ridge of Precambrian volcanic tuff. This volcanic tuff is a very fine-grained igneous rock. The individual crystals are almost invisible to the eye and it feels like fine sandpaper. About a tenth mile further west beyond the vegetable stand across from Bowles Terrace, the protruding highly stressed Precambrian Dedham Granite is hard to recognize. West of this outcrop, a valley without any outcropping rock runs from Lincoln north to Bloody Bluff in Lexington and south along the Lincoln/Weston border. On Route 117, this swale runs west from the Dedham Granite outcrop to first rock outcrop at the east end of Massachusetts Audubon Society's Drumlin Farm in Lincoln.

PARKING: Three parking areas are available.

1) Drive up Concord Road in Weston into Lincoln where it becomes Tower Road. Make the first left turn in Lincoln. This road is Stonehedge Road and it runs along a resistant rock outcrop, which is a part of the Bloody Bluff Fault system. Park just before reaching the turnaround at the end of Stonehedge Road by telephone pole number 134/20. Near this pole there is a stake marked TRAIL. If you follow this trail for about 200 feet, you will come to junction **9** in Weston.

2) One may park just beyond 133 Sudbury Road on a pull-out next to a path entering the Town Forest.

3) One may park just beyond 149 Sudbury Road
   by the gate to a fire road. Don't block the
   gate.

RECOMMENDED WALK:
This walk requires an hour and one-half to two
hours and looks at parts of the Bloody Bluff
Fault system which are displayed here.

Park in the parking place just beyond 133
Sudbury Road. The area just north of the road is
a old borrow pit possibly used for fill at the time
the road was built. Enter the pine plantation on
a path marked by an F & T arrow. The forest
floor here is covered with Canada mayflower or
wild lily-of-the-valley (*Maianthemum canadense*)
(Figure 25) and starflower (*Trientalis borealis*)
(Figure 27) in May. The path bears right, passes
through a stone wall, and then bears left leaving
the pine plantation. Continue straight ahead
ignoring the path to the right. Here, where more
light reaches the forest floor under the
hardwoods, one can find partridgeberry
(*Mitchella repens*) (Figure 28) which blooms in
early July.

The path comes to a fire road. Take the road to
your right into a mixed woodland. The road
rises and soon reaches junction **8**. At junction **8**,
follow the fire road to your left. As you follow
the fire road, you will note that you are walking
between two ridges. Here the bedrock outcrops
are a volcanic tuff like that along Route 117. You

may also note that the mid-story trees in this area include many hemlocks.

The fire road soon reaches junction **5**. Bear left and follow the road to junction **4**. At junction **4**, bear right and continue along a road. Again, as you descend along the road, you will find yourself in a hemlock grove with ridges with bedrock outcrops on either side of the road. These ridges diminish in height as the road ends at junction **3**.

At the left side of this junction, there is a sign, which reads:

LOW IMPACT HARVESTING

The wood harvesting in this forest is being done using low impact logging techniques. These methods are an integral part of Land's Sake approach to managing forests in an ecologically sustainable manner.

METHODS OF LOW IMPACT HARVESTING:

1. Directional Felling — Trees are cut to fall in directions that minimize damage to remaining overstory and understory trees.

2. Shedding and Winching — Once the trees are felled they are limbed and bucked (cut) into lengths ranging from 4 to 16 feet. The logs are then winched or pulled and bunched into

piles along temporary skid trails where they will be split into firewood or skidded to a sawmill site.

3. Slash — the branches, limbs, and tops of felled trees are called slash. These remains can be one of the most unsightly aspects of a logging job. To make the harvesting more aesthetically pleasing to recreational users, Land's Sake cuts the slash to less than two feet in height.

4. Skid trails — The skid trails coincide with the already existing trail and fire road network in this area. After the firewood has been removed the skid trails are no longer used and will regenerate with forest tree and plant species.

Through these low impact methods, Land's Sake makes it possible to harvest forest products, and to enjoy the beauty of the woods at the same time.

The area to the west of this sign to the Wayland border was harvested in the winter of 1994.

At junction **3**, bear left on the road which descends into a swampy area and becomes a path. Be careful as it can be difficult to follow paths in this swamp

Fig 37

at certain times of the year. Keep right when the path splits at the edge of the swampy area and when it ends on another path. If the path is under water, then go to your left on a slightly drier path and take the first right. You are soon on drier land with evergreen, leatherleaf, or marginal woodfern (*Dryopteris marginalis*) (Figure 20) and with cinnamon fern (*Osmunda cinnamomea*) (Figure 4), one of the wetland marker plants in the swamp to the right. A red maple canopy is present in the swamps. A ridge soon comes into view on the left as the path rises. There is a path to the left that goes up to the top of the ridge. Just beyond this path, there is an orange sign on a tree that reads:

Going along the path for a short distance, we reach a swamp in which we can see cinnamon fern (*Osmunda cinnamomea*), jewelweed or spotted touch-me-not (*Impatiens capensis*) (Figure 37), sphagnum moss, and tussock sedge (*Carex stricta*). Hans van Leer, who once farmed near this area in Lincoln, lost a horse in this quicksand. The edge of the swamp is close to the Lincoln/Weston Town Line. In this area, the

swamp fills the swale just west of the Bloody
Bluff Fault system that was described earlier as
being between Bowles Terrace and the east end
of Drumlin Farm along Route 117.

Let's reverse our direction and return to the path
by the orange sign and climb the hill. The hill is
an outcrop of a resistant bedrock of the fault
system. The trees are mainly black (or red) oaks.
Avoid the paths leading to the left and keep
along the top of the hill. The path descends
along a borrow pit. This borrow pit was used as
a rifle range during World War II. The path
levels out and reaches a fire road near a stone
wall, which is on the Wayland/Weston Town
Line. The meadow in Wayland is a property of
the Sudbury Valley Trustees. It is a pleasant
place to rest for a moment in the sun and have a
snack. (Remember: take your candy wrapper
and other trash back home for disposal. Respect
our wild land!) Often, a broad-winged or red-
tailed hawk will drift in the air above the
meadow.

Return to the opening in the stone wall and
follow the fire road to the east. The fire road was
the southerly boundary of the van Leer Farm
that extended north to Massachusetts Audubon
Society's Drumlin Farm Sanctuary. The road
gradually rises until it reaches junction **2**. As you
walk toward the junction notice that there is a
ravine on your right. This ravine is one of the
outlets of the glacial Lake Sudbury.

By the junction, there is a sign that reads:

WILDLIFE HABITAT ENHANCEMENT

This forest project uses sound silvicultural practices to maximize the wildlife potential of this woodlot. Increasing habitat diversity is the key to creating an area attractive to a wide array of animal species. Our work site will become a habitat "island" surrounded by more homogenous secondary growth woodland. Animals have four basic needs to sustain life.

1. Food — Forest thinning increases the available sunlight allowing the remaining trees to produce valuable food such as acorns and pine nuts. Berry bushes and tender herbaceous growth flourish with more space and light. Associated with this burst of growth is an increase in insect abundance, an important food source for many animals.

2. Cover — The forest provides sites to nest and rest and gives protection from weather and predators. New growth combined with brushy slash will offer thick ground cover. The hemlock grove has been preserved. Den and cavity trees are left standing as these provide natural holes for the use of birds and mammals.

3. Water — Logging activity has been kept out of wetland areas and our low-impact harvesting methods maintain soil integrity to

prevent erosion. Therefore water quality is kept high and this is especially important for the resident amphibians.

4. Space — Wildlife needs space to support healthy populations. This fifteen acre cutting area lies within a very extensive tract of contiguous conservation land.

The open character of this woodland provides an excellent opportunity for wildlife observation. Trail users may enjoy seeing a Great-crested Flycatcher with a mouth full of insects for its nestlings, catch a glimpse of white-tailed deer bounding away at dusk or even see a fox dinning on an eastern cottontail.

Please report interesting wildlife sightings to Land's Sake (781) 893 1162.

Bear left from junction **2**. Keep bearing right when the fire road reaches a wetland. Note that the presence of our wetland indicator plant cinnamon fern and that, at this site, it is accompanied by interrupted fern (*Osmunda claytoniana*) (Figure 5). Interrupted fern is recognized by the fact that its leaves often show a pattern on the stems of green sterile leaves, deep green or brown fertile leaves, and ending with green sterile leaves. Beyond the wetland, the path becomes a road that rises to reach junction **3**.

Continue straight ahead from junction **3**, avoiding the road at the right. In about 60 feet you reach a junction. The path going left enters Lincoln. Paths in Lincoln are usually marked with red plastic circles or rectangles which are often accompanied by a red diamond which indicate those parts of Lincoln's Trail System closed to bicycles. Bear right keeping in Weston. The wood is drier here; bracken fern borders the path. The path rises as it passes a resistant section of volcanic tuff along the Bloody Bluff Fault. In about 170 feet, we come to a junction. Turn right along a narrow path that rises as it heads to the south. The trees are largely a mixture of pine and black (or red) oak and the understory plants are mainly members of the heath family. At the height of land, take the path to your left that goes east rather than continuing to the south. This path continues to rise for about 25 feet and then slowly descends passing through a stone wall into a pine plantation. To your right, there are wetlands. Soon, on the left, some houses in Lincoln come into view and then you reach junction **9**.

Just to your left at junction **9**, there is a path leading northeast. This path marked with a large No Bikes sign and with a white arrow on a red rectangle leads to the parking place on Stonehedge Road in Lincoln.

To continue on our route, bear right at junction **9**. The houses in Lincoln remain in view with an occasional trail from their yards. The trail bears to the right just before reaching a vernal pool, rises over a low ridge, and then gradually descends. About 150 feet beyond the vernal pool site, there is a junction. At this junction, bear to the right. The path slowly descends and crosses an intermittent stream. These wetlands are the breeding place of several species of amphibians and invertebrates. Just beyond the stream, the trail follows an esker. An esker is a glacial deposit in the form of a winding ridge that formed from deposits of a stream that once flowed within the glacial ice. On either side of the esker, there are wetlands. Note that in this wetland area, the canopy trees include red maples and that the understory has cinnamon fern. At junction Y, avoid a path on the left going into the wetlands. Red maples disappear from the canopy when we reach drier woods.

The path reaches a fire road at junction **6**. Head left (southwest) along the fire road. Note the bed rock outcrop of volcanic tuff on your right. As you continue, another fire road enters from the left and 60 feet beyond you reach junction **7**. Avoid the path going to the right here, and continue going straight ahead. On the right side of the path, there are the remains of two pre-World War II vehicles. In about 150 feet beyond junction **7**, turn to the right on a path leading into a pine plantation. The path rises and passes around a bedrock outcrop to your right. Bearing to the right, the path descends, crosses 10 to 15 feet of wetland. This wetland has examples of cinnamon and interrupted fern plus another wetland indicator plant, royal fern (*Osmunda regalis*) (Figure 6). The path then rises into a pine plantation and reaches the path that we used to enter the forest. Turn left, pass through a stone wall and bear left along a path running straight to the Sudbury Road parking place.

APPENDIXES

Appendix A

WOODLAND FLOWERS

Spring is the best time of the year to find woodland wildflowers in Weston's woods. From mid-February, when the first skunk cabbage bloom may appear, until early July, when the partridgeberry blooms, you can find a succession of bloom in our woods.

Like all plants, woodland plants require only a few resources to grow: a supply of air and water, a few minerals from the soil, and light. Light is important to plants as it furnishes the energy necessary for their existence. Using the energy of the sunlight, most plants can take carbon dioxide (CO_2) from the air and water (H_2O) from the soil converting these substances into sugars which are the basic energy supplies used to maintain all living organisms. The process by which CO_2 and H_2O are converted to carbohydrate is known as photosynthesis.

The sugars resulting from photosynthesis are used by living organisms as a source of energy and material for the synthesis of complex carbohydrates, proteins, and lipids. Thus, these sugars are commonly referred to as food. Since most plants can produce their own food, scientists refer to plants as "autotrophes". Plants tend to grow best when conditions for photosynthesis are optimal.

Chlorophyll, which traps the energy of sunlight, is the green pigment found mainly in the leaves of plants. Notice how plant leaves spread to catch as much sunlight as possible. The better the spread of the leaves and the more light that falls upon the plant, the greater the amount of energy that can be captured to make food. When too little light falls upon a plant, the plant either will go dormant or die because it is unable to make sufficient supplies of food.

Plants produce flowers to reproduce. The reproductive organs of flowering plants are found in the flowers. Many flowers contain both female and male organs; however, some plants, such as the red maple, produce flowers that are either female or male. Many flowers are highly colored and scented, characteristics that attract insects and other pollinators as well as people.

As insects travel from flower to flower, they carry pollen from one plant to another. Under the right conditions, a pollen grain from one flower deposited on the stamen on another flower results in the male sperm growing into the ovary of the second flower resulting in fertilization. Each flower has evolved to attract specific pollinators that the flower smears with pollen for transport to another flower of the same species.

Plants use a large amount of food to produce flowers. To flower, a plant must be able to produce excess food by photosynthesis. To photosynthesize, a plant must have the maximum exposure to light. Why then do the woodland plants not flower in mid-summer when there is 16 hours of daylight and the weather is at its warmest? What is the advantage to flowering in the spring when there is less daylight and the weather is cooler?

Think a moment. Woodland plants grow on the forest floor under the trees. If the flowers bloom before the trees are fully leafed out, then these woodland plants are blooming when the maximum amount of light is reaching the forest floor.

The forest trees come into leaf about mid-May and begin to trap light for photosynthesis. These trees have an impressive spread of leaves to enable them to produce the food required to maintain their large size. By June, when most tree leaves have opened, the forest floor is darker and cooler than a nearby sunny meadow.

Once the trees in a forest are in leaf, insufficient light reaches the forest floor to allow most plants there to produce excess food. Some, such as the Turks' cap and wood lilies, are able to grow and blossom under the trees. Others, such as partridgeberry and the members of the wintergreen family, which are evergreen and store energy throughout the year, are able to bloom during July. However, the flowers of the partridgeberry and the wintergreen family members are only about a fourth to half inch in diameter and the plants are less than 6 inches high, so most people fail to notice their beauty. Most other woodland flowers simply die back and become dormant during the summer. Their chance to grow must await the bright light of the next spring. They survive until then as seeds, bulbs, or corms. A corm is an underground stem and that of the Bloodroot is very impressive with its reddish sap.

Parts of a woodland are normally dominated by one type of a tree, rather than a mixture of many species. The different types of a woodland support different types of flowers. Two of the main reasons for this observation are that the amount of light reaching the forest floor and that the time at which the leaves erupt depends upon the species. Oak trees have many gaps in the leaf coverage and tend to leaf out late. Many woodland flowers, such as the moccasin flower (pink lady slipper), are most easily found in an oak woods. The woodland floor in a beech woods is very dark since beech trees have a dense canopy of leaves which forms early in the spring. Few flowers are found under beeches other than beechdrops. A chlorophyll lacking parasite, which grows on beech roots, beechdrops flower during the early summer when the root sap is rich in photosynthesis products from the canopy. Look for beechdrops along the roots of beech trees in mid-summer.

Winter conditions are often hard on plants. Short days, low temperatures, and occasional blankets of snow make difficult conditions for maintaining photosynthesis. Thus many woodland plants and trees shed their leaves in the autumn and shut down for the winter.

Losing leaves is a strategy that also aids plants to survive under dry conditions. The thin, delicate structure of leaves, so helpful in capturing light in the warmth of summer, is vulnerable to frost damage in the cold and winds of winter. Without leaves, a plant will lose less water, a factor of great importance if water is scarce because the ground is frozen. Those plants which keep their leaves throughout the year either have needle-shaped leaves (pines) or roll their leaves into compact tubes (rhododendrons) to avoid water loss in the winter. Without leaves or with needle-like leaves, branches are less likely to become burdened with great weights of snow. In a typical deciduous woodland, light levels on the woodland floor rise during the winter and peak during late winter. It is this available light that is exploited by the woodland wildflowers. Their growth is timed between the worst conditions of winter and the time when the trees leaf out in late spring.

One way that woodland wildflowers are able to survive the winter is by producing seeds. Seeds are the result of the pollinator supported sexual activity that occurred in the flowers of the previous spring. The seeds contain a new plant and a supply of food. (Examine a peanut. The peanut heart can be recognized as a small plant; the two halves of the "nut" are a food supply.) When conditions are appropriate, the stored food supply supports the growth of the new plant. Many seeds have evolved so that an extended cold period is required before the new plant will grow. This adaptation prevents the plant from growing during October and November and then freezing to death in December and January.

Another way that woodland flowers survive is to store excess energy in a bulb or a corm. As the trees leaf out, the plant continues photosynthesis until too little light is available. It then dies back having stored food in seeds and/or in its bulb or corm. Like seeds, bulbs, or corms must undergo a cold period before they can use their stored food to produce a new plant in the following spring. The stored food must be sufficient to support the formation of new leaves so that the plant can resume photosynthesis.

This well-adapted system is in peril if people disturb or pick the woodland wildflowers. Although it might seem that cutting or picking flowers, but leaving the rest of a plant, would allow the plant to survive, survival is not guaranteed. Trampling the ground around the wildflower may damage its bulb, corm, or roots. Removing the upper part of a plant may reduce the quantity of energy trapped by photosynthesis so that insufficient food will be produced in the leaves for storage in the bulb, corm, or roots to enable regrowth in the following season.

Wildflowers can remain dormant for many years. When a woodland is carefully cut back, sufficient light may penetrate to the forest floor to restart growth. Seeds, bulbs, and corms, which have been dormant, can suddenly spring back to life.

Many different flowers may appear in an area that was dark and gloomy before cutting. The number of different flower species may give an indication of how long ago a particular area was cleared. The older the wood, the greater the chance that a species of flower has become established.

Woodland flowers that survive as either bulbs or corms tend to be found in the same place each year. These plants are often not prolific producers of seed. Thus, the movement of these plants to new sites is very slow. Newer woodlands often have only a few species of woodland flowers and often have some meadow flowers.

In Weston, woodland wildflowers are most often found on shaded hillsides and banks which have not been cleared recently for fields, pastures, or building sites. As most of the present woodlands in Weston have grown up either after the 1938 hurricane or since farming ceased after World War II, native wildflowers are beginning to reestablish themselves in undisturbed areas.

Appendix B

MONTH BY MONTH CALENDAR OF BLOOM
WESTON, MASSACHUSETTS

This calendar of bloom is based upon my records over many years. Dates are given by month and week. Thus, 3/4 means March during the fourth week.

Scientific name	Common name(s)	Flowering Begins	Ends
MARCH			
Symplocarpus foetidus	Skunk cabbage	3/2	4/4
Salix glaucophylloides	Broadleaf willow	3/4	4/4
APRIL			
Lindera benzoin	Spicebush	4/2	5/2
Sanguinaria canadensis	Bloodroot	4/2	5/2
Tussilago farfara	Coltsfoot	4/2	5/1
Acer rubrum	Red or swamp maple	4/2	4/4
Claytonia caroliniana	Spring beauty	4/3	5/2
Erythronium americanum	Yellow trout lily	4/3	5/2
Antennaria sp.	Pussytoes	4/4	6/2
Caltha palustris	Marsh marigold	4/4	5/3
Claytonia virginica	Spring beauty	4/4	5/3
Coptis groenlandica	Goldthread	4/4	6/2
Uvularia sessilifolia	Wild oats or Sessile-leaved bellwort	4/4	5/3
Waldsteinia fragarioides	Barren strawberry	4/4	5/3
MAY			
Arctostapylos uva-ursi	Bearberry	5/1	5/4
Clintonia borealis	Bluebead lily	5/2	5/4
Calycanthus fertilis	Smooth allspice	5/2	5/4
Cornus canadensis	Bunchberry	5/2	6/3
Geranium maculatum	Wild geranium	5/2	6/2
Ledum groenlandicum	Labrador tea	5/2	6/3
Podophyllum peltatum	Mayapple or mandrake	5/2	5/4
Polygala paucifolia	Fringed polygala	5/2	5/4
Polygonatum pubescens	Hairy Solomon's seal	5/2	5/4
Smilacina racemosa	Wild spikenard or false Solomon's seal	5/2	5/4
Trillium cernuum	Nodding trillium	5/2	5/4
Uvularia perfoliata	Bellwort or strawbell	5/2	6/2
Cypripedum acaule	Pink lady's slipper or Moccasin Flower	5/3	6/2
Houstonia caerulea	Quaker ladies, Innocence, or Bluets	5/3	6/2
Polygonatum biflorum	Smooth Solomon's seal	5/3	5/4

Viola pedata	Bird's foot violet	5/3	6/2
Cornus kousa	Kousa dogwood	5/4	7/2
Krigia virginica	Dwarf dandelion	5/4	7/2
Lychnis flos-cuculi	Ragged robin	5/4	7/3

JUNE

Hieracium venosum	Rattlesnake weed	6/1	6/3
Medeola virginica	Indian cucumber root	6/1	6/3
Meehania cordata	Creeping mint	6/1	7/1
Corydalis sempervirens	Pink or pale corydalis or		
	Rock harlequin	6/2	10/1
Erigeron annuus	Daisy fleabane	6/2	7/3
Michella repens	Partridgeberry	6/2	7/1
Sisyrinchium sp.	Blue-eyed grass	6/2	7/2
Veratrum viride	False or white hellebore or		
	Indian poke	6/2	6/3
Veronica serpyllifolia	Thyme-leaved speedwell	6/2	9/3
Ilex verticillata	Winterberry	6/3	7/1
Rosa virginiana	Virginia rose	6/3	7/3

JULY

Lysimachia quarrifolia	Whorled loosestrife	7/1	7/4
Lysimachia terrestris	Swamp loosestrife	7/1	7/4
Melanpyrum lineare	Cow wheat	7/1	7/4
Chimaphila maculata	Stripped pipsissewa,		
	Stripped or		
	Spotted Wintergreen	7/2	7/4
Hypericum perforatum	Common St. Johnswort	7/2	8/2
Spirea tomentosa	Steeplebush	7/2	8/2
Chimaphila umbellata	Pipsissewa	7/3	8/1
Clethra alnifolia	Sweet pepperbush	7/3	9/1
Lobelia cardinalis	Cardinal flower	7/4	10/4

AUGUST

Cephalantus occidentalis	Buttonbush	8/1	8/4
Eupatorium purpureum	Joe Pye weed	8/2	9/2
Impatiéns glandulifera	Jewelweed	8/2	9/2
Polygonum cuspidatum	Japanese knotweed	8/4	10/2
Aster novae-angliae	New England aster	8/4	10/3

SEPTEMBER

Aster cordifolius	Heartleaved aster	9/1	9/4
Aster linariifolius	Bristly aster	9/1	10/3
Aster novi-belgii	New York aster	9/4	10/4

APPENDIX C

Author's List of Weston Wildlife

This list is reconstructed from memory and includes only those species that I have personally observed from 1957 through the present. The sequence in each list follows the order used in the various scientific Checklists, which places species in the sequence of their presumed natural relationships. For example, birds are listed in the order of the American Ornithologists' Union (A. O. U.) 1983 Check-list as modified for the National Geographic Society <u>Field Guide to the Birds of North America</u>, 1983. The appropriate Checklist used for the other Classes of Phylum Chordata can be found by checking the field guide used for the specific class the bibliography.

<u>MAMMALS</u>

Opossum (*Didelphis marsupalis*)
Masked shrew (*Sorex cinereus*)
Shorttail shrew (*Blarina brevicauda*)
Starnosed mole (*Condyluria cristata*)
Little brown bat (*Myotis lucifugus*)
Hoary bat (*Lasiurus cinereus*)
Shortailed weasel (*Mustela erminea*)
Raccoon (*Procyon lotor*)
River otter (*Lutra canadensis*)
Striped skunk (*Mephitis mephitis*)
Red fox (*Vulpes fulva*)

Woodchuck (*Marmota monax*)
Eastern chipmunk (*Tamias striatus*)
Red squirrel (*Tamiasciurus hudsonicus*)
Eastern grey squirrel (*Sciurus carolinensis*)
Southern flying squirrel (*Glaucomys volans*)
White-footed mouse (*Peromyscus leucopus*)
Eastern woodrat (*Neotoma floridana*)
Boreal redback vole (*Clethrionomys rutilus*)
Meadow vole (*Microtus pennsylvanicus*)
Muskrat (*Ondatra zibethica*)
Eastern cottontail (*Sylvilgus floridanus*)
Whitetail deer (*Odocoileus virginianus*)

BIRDS

Pied-billed grebe (*Podilymbus podiceps*)
Horned grebe (*Podiceps auritus*)
Great cormorant (*Phalacrocorax carbo*)
Double-crested cormorant (*Phalacorcorax auritus*)
Great blue heron (*Ardea herodias*)
Green-backed heron (*Butorides striatus*)
Mute swan (*Cygnus olor*)
Canada goose (*Branta canadensis*)
Mallard duck (*Anas platyrhynchoss*)
American black duck (*Anas rubripes*)
Gadwall (*Anas strepera*)
Green-winged teal (*Anas crecca*)
Blue-winged teal (*Anas discors*)
Shoveller (*Anas clypeata*)
Wood duck (*Aix sponsa*)
Ring-necked duck (*Aythya collaris*)
Common goldeneye (*Bucephala clangula*)
Bufflehead (*Bucephala albeola*)

Hooded merganser (*Laphodytes cucullatus*)
Common merganser (*Mergus merganser americanus*)
Killdeer (*Charadrius vociferus*)
Spotted Sandpiper (*Actitis macularia*)
American Woodcock (*Scolopax minor*)
Ring-billed gull (*Larus delawarensis*)
Herring gull (*Larus argentatus*)
Great black-backed gull (*Larus marinus*)
Turkey vulture (*Cathartes aura*)
Sharp-shinned hawk (*Accipiter stratus*)
Cooper's hawk (*Accipiter cooperii*)
Goshawk (*Accipiter gentilis*)
Red-shouldered hawk (*Buteo lineatus*)
Broad-winged hawk (*Buteo platypterus*)
Red-tailed hawk (*Buteo jamaicensis*)
Osprey (*Pandion haliaetus*)
American kestrel (*Falco sparverius*)
Merlin (*Falco columbarius*)
Ruffed grouse (*Bonasa umbellus*)
Northern bobwhite (*Colinus virginianus*)
Ring-necked pheasant (*Phasianus colchicus*)
Turkey (*Meleagris gallopavo*)
Rock dove (*Columba livia*)
Mourning dove (*Zenaida macrora*)
Black-billed cuckoo (*Coccyzus erythropthalmus*)
Great horned owl (*Bubo virginianus*)
Barred owl (*Strix varia*)
Eastern screech-owl (*Otus asio*)
Common nighthawk (*Chordeiles minor*)
Chimney swift (*Chaetura pelagica*)
Ruby-throated hummingbird (*Archilochus colubris*)
Belted kingfisher (*Ceryle alcyon*)

Red-bellied woodpecker (*Melanerpes carolinus*)
Northern flicker (*Colaptes auratus*)
Yellow-bellied sapsucker (*Sphyrapicus varius*)
Downy woodpecker (*Picoides pubescens*)
Hairy woodpecker (*Picoides villosus*)
Pileated woodpecker (*Dryocopus pileatus*)
Eastern kingbird (*Tyrannus tryannus*)
Great crested flycatcher (*Myiarchus crinitus*)
Eastern wood-pewee (*Contopus virens*)
Eastern phoebe (*Sayornis phoebe*)
Least flycatcher (*Empidonax minmus*)
Horned lark (*Eremophila alpestris*)
Tree swallow (*Tachycineta bicolor*)
Bank swallow (*Riparia riparia*)
Barn swallow (*Hiundo rustica*)
Blue jay (*Cyanocitta cristata*)
American crow (*Corvus brachyrhynchos*)
Tufted titmouse (*Parus bicolor*)
Black-capped chickadee (*Parus atricapillus*)
Brown creeper (*Certhia americana*)
White-breasted nuthatch (*Sitta carolinensis*)
Red-breasted nuthatch (*Sitta canadensis*)
House wren (*Troglodytes aedon*)
Winter wren (*Troglodytes troglodytes*)
Carolina wren (*Thryothorus ludovicianus*)
Golden-crowned kinglet (*Regulus satrapa*)
Ruby-crowned kinglet (*Regulus calendula*)
Eastern bluebird (*Sialia sialis*)
Wood thrush (*Hylocichia mustelina*)
Veery (*Catharus fusescens*)
Hermit thrush (*Catharus guttatus*)
American robin (*Turdus migratorius*)
Gray catbird (*Dumetella carolinensis*)
Northern mockingbird (*Mimus polyglottos*)

Brown thrasher (*Toxostoma rufum*)
Cedar waxwing (*Bombycilla cedorum*)
European starling (*Sturnus vulgaris*)
Solitary vireo (*Vireo solitarius*)
Red-eyed vireo (*Vireo olivaceus*)
Warbling vireo (*Vireo gilvus*)
Blue-winged warbler (*Vermivora pinus*)
Northern parula (*Parula americana*)
Black-and-white warbler (*Mniotilta varia*)
Black-throated blue warbler (*Dendroica caerulescens*)
Blackburnian warbler (*Dendroica fusca*)
Chestnut-sided warbler (*Dendroica pensylvanica*)
Magnolia warbler (*Dendroica magnolia*)
Yellow-rumped warbler (*Dendroica coronata*)
Black-throated green warbler (*Dendroica virens*)
Pairie warbler (*Dendroica discolor*)
Blackpoll warbler (*Dendroica striata*)
Pine warbler (*Dendroica pinus*)
Palm warbler (*Dendroica palmarum*)
Yellow warbler (*Dendroica petechia*)
Canada warbler (*Oporornis formosus*)
Ovenbird (*Seiurus aurocapillus*)
Northern waterthrush (*Seiurus noveboracensis*)
Common yellowthroat (*Geothlypis trichas*)
American redstart (*Setophaga ruticilla*)
Rose-breasted grosbeak (*Pheucticus ludovicianus*)
Northern cardinal (*Cardinalis cardinalis*)
Indigo bunting (*Passerina cyanea*)
Rufous-sided towhee (*Piplo erythrophthalmus*)
Savannah sparrow (*Passerculus sandwichensis*)
Song sparrow (*Melospiza melodia*)
American tree sparrow (*Spizella arborea*)
Field sparrow (*Spizella pusilla*)

Chipping sparrow (*Spizella passerina*)
Dark-eyed junco (*Junco hyemalis*)
White-throated sparrow (*Zonotrichia albicollis*)
Fox sparrow (*Passerella iliaca*)
Swamp sparrow (*Melospiza georgiana*)
Bobolink (*Dolichonyx oryzivorus*)
Eastern meadowlark (*Sturnella magna*)
Red-winged blackbird (*Agelaius phoeniceus*)
Rusty blackbird (*Euphagus carolinus*)
Brown-headed cowbird (*Molothrus ater*)
Common grackle (*Quiscalus quiscula*)
Orchard oriole (*Icterus spurius*)
Baltimore oriole (*Icterus galbula*)
Scarlet tanager (*Piranga olivacea*)
House sparrow (*Passer domesticus*)
Pine siskin (*Carduelis pinus*)
American goldfinch (*Carduelis tristis*)
Red crossbill (*Loxia curvirostra*)
White-winged crossbill (*Loxia leucoptera*)
Pine grosbeak (*Pinicola enucleator*)
Common redpoll (*Carduelis flammea*)
Purple finch (*Carpodacus purpureus*)
House finch (*Carpodacus mexicanus*)
Evening grosbeak (*Coccothausles vespertinus*)

REPTILES

Snapping turtle (*Chelydra serpentina*)
Spotted turtle (*Clemnys guttata*)
Eastern box turtle (*Terrapene carolina carolina*)
Eastern painted turtle (*Chrysemys picta picta*)
Eastern garter snake (*Thamnophis sirtalis sirtalis*)
Northern water snake (*Natrix sipedon sipedon*)

AMPHIBIANS

Spotted salamander (*Ambystoma serpentina*)
Red-spotted newt (*Diemictylus viridescens viridescens*)
Red-backed salamander (*Plethodon cinerus cinerus*)
American toad (*Bufo americanus*)
Fowler's toad (*Bufo woodhousi fowleri*)
Spring peeper (*Hyla crucifer*)
Bullfrog (*Rana catesbeiana*)
Green frog (*Rana clamitans melanota*)
Northern leopard frog (*Rana pipens pipens*)
Pickerel frog (*Rana palustris*)
Wood frog (*Rana sylvatica*)

FISH

I am not a fisherman. However, I have been shown brook, brown, and rainbow trout by those who fish our brooks. Pickerel are found in the pond at the eastern end of the Sears Land.

INVERTEBRATES

I have not maintained a listing of all invertebrates that I have identified over the years by using various field guides. However, a summary of some observations is given below.

The Allegheny Mound Ants (Formica exsectoides) and their mounds are found in the Jericho town Forest.

Many undisturbed ponds have crayfish which are indicators of pure water.

Vernal pools contain fresh water sponges, fairy shrimp, and fresh water clams.

Most common pond insects can be found in the ponds throughout town.

Appendix D

HISTORICAL NOTE CONCERNING WESTON CONSERVATION LAND

In 1950, there were fewer than 1200 dwellings in Weston. Of the 10,760 acres of land in the Town, there were 38 acres of parks, 25 acres of municipal land, and three reservoirs. In 1953, on the recommendation of the Selectmen and the Planning Board, the Town voted to establish a Committee to Investigate and Report on the Matter of a Town Forest (CIRMTF). The CIRMFT was enlarged in 1954. In 1955, the Town unanimously voted to appropriate sixty-five thousand dollars to acquire some 200 to 250 acres of land as recommended by CIRMTF. In the course of its deliberations, CIRMTF consulted with the Massachusetts Forest and Park Association and the newly established Sudbury Valley Trustees. These organizations recommended setting up a citizen organization to support the Town Forest Committee. The Town Forest Committee was independent of CIRMTF and managed the Town Forest. Thus, the Weston Forest and Trail Association was incorporated in 1955 as an educational group under Chapter 180 which enables the incorporation of nonprofit and charitable organizations. The Association's mission is to develop and maintain the system of trails in the Town and to encourage the study of nature and conservation. Major functions of the Association have been its monthly trail walk the first Sunday of each month from October through June and the Annual Lecture which have served to help educate residents of the value of maintaining conservation land. The Association has always mailed its annual report to all citizens of the Town as a part of it education effort. The Association has had a long-standing policy of helping the Town acquire land, which either because of the lack of sufficient time or funds, the Town would have not been able to obtain.

The founders of the Forest and Trail Association were:

> Marie E. Lewis, president
> William A. Elliston, clerk
> Henrietta N. Paine, treasurer
> Thomas D. Cabot
> Roger E. Ela
> Florence E. Freeman
> Stanley G. French
> Francis G. Goodale
> Victor C. Harnish
> Ellen R. Lempereur
> John B. Paine, Jr.
> Harrison S. Ripley

William A. Elliston, the heart of the organization for nearly thirty years, and many other members of the Forest and Trail Association have had a major role in the protection of the open space which we now enjoy.

The first two steps were taken in December 1955. The Town purchased about 150 acres from the Paine Trustees to establish the Highland Street Town Forest. Gifts have added to this Town Forest; a five acre parcel with frontage on Highland Street which provides a view to the west was given by members of the Paine Family in memory of General and Mrs. Charles Jackson Paine and their sons. During the next four years, Mrs. Marion Farnsworth Boynton donated 41.6 acres of land that initiated the Jericho Town Forest. Further gifts and purchases have resulted in Jericho being the largest Town Forest with an area of 550 acres. In 1957, the Recreation Commission purchased the Cat Rock area from the Cat Rock Trust.

In 1960, the Town voted to establish a permanent Open Areas Committee replacing the CIRMTF. In 1961, the Conservation Commission, established as a result of a new law, took over the function of the Open Areas Committee as well as the management of the wetlands. In 1972, the Town voted to accept the Germeshausen-Uyterhoeven proposal to authorize bond issues of up to $ 2.8 million for the acquisition of conservation land. An additional $ 1.3 million was voted two years later. When Weston College was converted to the Campion Center in 1977, the Town purchased 146 acres of former college land, including College Pond. The Town sought outside funds for the first time in this transaction. Some funds were obtained from the

Massachusetts Self-Help Program. In 1986, the Town voted a $3.8 million bond issue to purchase Case Field, the centrally located 48 acres of the former Case Estates land owned by Harvard University's Arnold Arboretum.

In 1989, the Town Forest Committee was dissolved and its functions were transferred to the Conservation Commission. At present, there is no administrative distinction between Town Conservation Land and Town Forest. In 1997, there are 1740 acres of Town Conservation land (16 % of the Town's area), 31 acres of Town Parks, and 107 acres of Town Recreation Land. In addition, the Weston Forest and Trail Association owns 134 acres of land and holds 14 acres of conservation easements plus 15 miles of trail easements.

In the purchase of Conservation Land, the initial policy was to purchase mainly undevelopable land. Hilltops were purchased as they are usually bedrock outcrops and require great engineering effort to establish a house site. Wetlands and streams were purchased as they are catchment areas for the water supply of Cambridge and of Wellesley. Wetlands and streams are esthetically attractive and important habitat for flowers and for wildlife. In 1990's, there has been an effort to preserve important viewscapes.

Appendix E

Trail User's Guide
to Weston Conservation Land

The Weston Conservation Commission and the Weston Forest and Trail Association encourage you to enjoy the open space maintained and made available for your use by these organizations. Brochures and Maps are available at the Town Hall (Engineer's Office). Maintenance and development of these trails, lands, and outlooks is made possible by membership dues and contributions to the Weston Forest and Trail Association, as well as funds provided by the Weston Conservation Commission. Membership in the Forest and Trail Association is not limited to Weston Residents.

In order to preserve the natural character of the trails and woods in Weston, the Weston Conservation Commission and the Weston Forest and Trail Association asks you to **please observe and respect the following rules:**

1) The Trails are intended to be used only for walking, jogging, cross-country skiing, and horseback riding. The operation of motorbikes, snowmobiles, and other motorized vehicles is not allowed.

2) **The following is forbidden** on Weston
   Conservation lands:

   Use of alcoholic beverages;
   disturbing the peace; carrying of
   firearms; hunting of animals and
   birds; damaging, removing, or
   cutting of any kind of trees, shrubs,
   flowers, signs, structures, or
   natural features; discarding of
   waste materials of any kind;
   lighting fires without the written
   permission from the Weston
   Conservation Commission and the
   Weston Fire Department

3) **We also ask you to please be mindful of
   the following guidelines:**

   - Bicyclists should mainly use the
     fire roads as shown on the trail
     map.
   - Bicycle riding is discouraged on
     hillsides or in wet weather
     when the ground is soft.
   - Horseback riding is
     discouraged when trails are wet
     and subject to severe damage.
   - Bicycle and horseback riding can
     be dangerous, and we request that
     riders be courteous and attentive to
     other trail users.

Helpful suggestions for everyone's enjoyment

1. If you bring food, please take all waste and packaging out again with you.

2. If you see paper, cans, bottles, or other trash along the trails or in the woods, help us by picking them up and depositing them in an appropriate receptacle when you come out of the woods.

3. If you see downed trees or branches which obstruct the trails, please drop us a note or call (781) 235 4195, so we can keep the trails in good shape.

4. Do not make fires or cut trees or branches, or pick wildflowers. (See "Rules")

5. We welcome your suggestions or comments, to make these trails more enjoyable to all.

For Trail Bicycle Riders:

Bicycle Riders should conform to the rules of the NEMBA (New England Mountain Bike Association, P.O. Box 380557, Cambridge, MA 02238). This association publishes a booklet entitled "SHARE THE TRAILS" which includes the following recommendations:

- Ride only on existing trails, don't make new ones.

- Respect private property.

- Never litter.

- Try to pack out more than you bring in.

- Never ride when and where you will leave ruts.

- Carry your bike through streams.

- Be careful not to widen trails by riding over vegetation alongside the trail.

- Don't skid. Don't brake slide...this can degrade hills by forming gullies that water funnels down, and can create ruts in sensitive trails.

- Respect Nordic ski tracks by staying off of the snow-covered cross-country ski trails.

- Hikers have the right of way, so slow down, stop, or pull to the side of the trail when encountering persons on foot.

- Remember that it is your responsibility to insure your use of the trails does not spoil that of other trail users, or spoil the trails themselves.

Resting

BIBLIOGRAPHY

1993. Preliminary Report of the Crescent Street Historical District Study Committee. Weston, Massachusetts: unpublished. An interesting historical study of Crescent Street and its dwellings.

Barosh, Patrick J. 1984. The Bloody Bluff Fault System. Paper of the 76th Annual New England Intercollegiate Geologic Conference. Geology of the Coastal Lowlands Boston, MA to Kennebunk, ME. Edited by Lindley S. Hanson, Salem State College, Salem, MA

Barosh, Patrick J. 1984. Regional Geology and Tectonic History of Southeastern New England. Paper of the 76th Annual New England Intercollegiate Geologic Conference. Geology of the Coastal Lowlands Boston, MA to Kennebunk, ME. Edited by Lindley S. Hanson, Salem State College, Salem, MA

Bates, George P. 1985. The Nathaniel Jennison House (1732). Weston Library Historical Collection.

Blamey, Marjorie; Fitter, Richard; and Fitter, Alastair. 1978. The Wild Flowers of Britain and Northern Europe, Third Edition. London, England: Collins, St. James's Place. This guide is arranged by family and is a handy adjunct to native plant guides as it works for many of the front lawn weeds. Our forebears brought many seeds with them from Europe.

Boston & Maine Railroad Historical Society. 1975. The Central Mass. Reading Massachusetts.

Brown, Lauren. 1979. Grasses. Boston, Massachusetts: Houghton Mifflin Company.

Burt, William Henry and Grossenheider, Richard Phillip. 1964. A Field Guide of the Mammals. Second Edition. Boston, Massachusetts: Houghton Mifflin Company.

Colburn, Philip F. 1981. Growing Up in Weston. Waltham, Massachusetts: Privately Printed. A collection of personal memories of a boyhood at the turn of the century.

Conant, Roger. 1958 A Field Guide to Reptiles and Amphibians of the United States and Canada East of the 100th Meridian. Boston, Massachusetts: Houghton Mifflin Company.

Dickson, Brenton H. 1963. Once Upon a Pung. Boston: Privately Printed. A collection of personal memories prepared for the 250th anniversary of the incorporation of Weston.

Dickson, Brenton H. 1977. Random Recollections. Weston, Massachusetts: Nobb

Hill Press, Inc. A collection of memories of childhood prepared for his grandchildren.

Dictionary of American Biography, Charles Schibner's Sons, New York.

Dirr, Michael A. 1990. Manual of Woody Landscape Plants. Champaign, Illinois: Stipes Publishing Company.

Fowler-Billings, Katharine. 1977. The Geological Story of Wellesley. The Wellesley Conservation Council, Inc.

Goldthwait, James Walker. 1905. The sand plains of glacial Lake Sudbury. Cambridge, Massachusetts: Harvard College Museum of Comparative Zoology Bulletin, v. 42, p 263-301.

Jorgensen, Neil. 1971. A Guide to New England's Landscape. Barre, Massachusetts: Barre Publishers. Part II, The Face of New England, is a thorough, non-technical account of glaciation, citing many New England examples. Part III, The Vegetation, is a thorough, non-technical account of the types of habitat found in New England.

Karr, Ronald Dale. 1989. Lost Railroads of New England. Pepperell, Massachusetts: Branch Line Press.

Karr, Ronald Dale. 1995. The Rail Lines of Southern New England. Pepperell, Massachusetts: Branch Line Press.

Kotoff, Carl. 1963. Glacial Lakes Near Concord, Massachusetts: Art. 96 in U.S. GEOL. SURVEY PROF. PAPER 475-C, pages C142-C144.

Kotoff, Carl. 1964. Surficial Geological Map of the Concord Quadrangle (GQ 331). Washington, D. C.: U.S. Geological Survey. A brief explanatory text with references accompanies this map.

Lamson, Colonel Daniel S. 1913. History of the Town of Weston, Massachusetts. Boston, Massachusetts: Geo. H. Ellis Co. The pictures of homes taken about 1900 show the surroundings as open farmland.

Murie, Olaus J. 1954. A Field Guide to Animal Tracks. Boston, Massachusetts: Houghton Mifflin Company. This guide is a favorite of mine. It discusses behavior and sign of each species. I also have had the privilege of spending several evenings working with the casts, pelts, skeletons, and other items of the Muries' collection in Jackson Hole and then walking wintry trail investigating sign which lead, in some cases, to the maker.

Nelson, Arthur E. 1974. Surficial Geological Map of the Natick Quadrangle (GQ 1151)

Washington, D.C.: U.S. Geological Survey. Brief explanatory text with references appears on this map.

Newcomb, Lawrence. 1977. Newcomb's Wildflower Guide. An Ingenious New Key System for Quick, Positive Field Identification of the Wildflowers, Flowering Shrubs and Vines of Northeastern and Northcentral North America. Boston, Massachusetts: Little, Brown and Company. Newcomb asks you to look at a plant and ask yourself five questions. The answer generates a three digit number, which leads you into his guide.

Open Space & Recreation Planning Committee. 1997. Open Space & Recreation Plan Resource Analysis for the Town of Weston, MA.

Pielou, E. C. 1991. After the Ice Age: the return of life to glaciated North America. Chicago, Illinois: The University of Chicago Press. Treats the last 20 thousand years of environmental change from several prospectives.

Peterson, Roger Tory and McKenny, Margaret. 1968. A Field Guide to Wildflowers of Northeastern and Northcentral North America. Boston, Massachusetts: Houghton Mifflin Company. This Peterson Guide uses a visual approach based on color, form, and detail.

Raymo, Chet and Raymo, Maureen E. 1989. Written in Stone. A Geological History of the Northeastern United States. Chester, Connecticut: The Globe Pequot Press. Includes maps, which show the evolution of the land area of our region.

Ripley, Emma F. 1961. Weston - A Puritan Town. Weston, Massachusetts: The Benevolent-Alliance of the First Parish.

Roberts, David C. 1996. A Field Guide to Geology. Eastern North America. Boston: Houghton Mifflin Company. Chapter 2 is a discussion of some basic geology, which is useful background when observing rocks. Plate 43 (1) shows a mylonite sample from a fault zone in Weston. Similiar mylonite samples can be found along the trails in Weston. Chapter 5, The Appalachian Province, treats the geology of our region. I recommend reading the introduction to this chapter, pages 219 and 220; The Lay of the Land, pages 220 and 221; The Rocks of the Appalachian Province, pages 221 and 222; The History of the Appalachian Province, page 222 to the top of page 229; Appalachian Zones and History, pages 246 and 247; The Triassic Basins, page 247 to near the bottom of page 250; The Northeastern Appalachians: New England, page 278 to the middle of page 285; Massachusetts and Connecticut, pages 289 and 290; The Avalonian Zone, page 290 to the top of page 294; and The Connecticut Valley Triassic Basin, page 295 and 296.

Shuttleworth, Floyd S. and Zim, Herbert S. 1967. Non-flowering Plants. New York: Golden Press.

Skehan, James W., S.J. 1979. Puddingstone, Drumlins and Ancient Volcanoes, a Geologic Field Guide along Historic Trails of Boston. Dedham, Massachusetts: WesStone Press. A layman's guide to the regional geology of the Boston area.

Symonds, George W. 1963. The Shrub Identification Book. The visual method for the practical identification of shrubs, including woody vines and ground covers. New York, New York: William Morrow and Company.

Symonds, George W. 1958. The Tree Identification Book. A new method for the practical identification and recognition of trees. New York, New York: William Morrow and Company.

Thompson, Margaret. 1982. Reading Ancient Landscapes. An approach to Geology Illustrated by Examples From Broadmoor Wildlife Sanctuary and Neighboring

Localities. Milford, Massachusetts: Charlescraft Press.

Van Diver, Bradford B. 1987. Roadside Geology of Vermont and New Hampshire. Missoula, Montana: Mountain Press Publishing Company.

Wiggers, Raymond 1994. The Plant Explorer's Guide to New England. Missoula, Montana: Mountain Press Publishing Company.

Table of Figures

Figure   Page